Why Women Aren't
Winning at Health
(but can)

WHY WOMEN AREN'T WINNING AT HEALTH

(but can)

Second Edition

Anca Griffiths
Alyson J. McGregor, MD
& Marjorie Jenkins, MD

WORLDCHANGERS
M E D I A

MEDICAL / Health Policy
HEALTH & FITNESS / Women's Health

DISCLAIMER: This is a work of nonfiction. Nonetheless, some of the names and identifying character traits of people featured in the stories herein have been changed in order to protect their identities. Any resulting resemblance to persons either living or dead is entirely coincidental.

The publisher and the Authors make no representations or warranties of any kind with respect to this book or its contents, and assume no responsibility for errors, inaccuracies, omissions, or any other inconsistencies herein. Although the authors are medical experts, the content of this book is for entertainment purposes only and is not intended to diagnose, treat, cure, or prevent any condition or disease, including mental health conditions. You understand that this book is not intended as a substitute for consultation with a licensed healthcare provider. The use of this book implies your acceptance of this disclaimer.

At the time of publication, the URLs displayed in this book refer to existing websites owned by Anca Griffiths/OM Experts, the contributing authors, and/or authors' affiliates. WorldChangers Media is not responsible for, nor should be deemed to endorse or recommend, these websites; nor is it responsible for any website content other than its own, or any content available on the internet not created by WorldChangers Media.

Second Edition
Hardcover: 978-1-955811-51-4
Paperback: 978-1-955811-52-1
E-book: 978-1-955811-53-8
LCCN: 2023924067

Second hardcover edition: January 2024
First hardcover edition: May 2023

Cover artwork: Renata Jessiman
Layout and typesetting: Bryna Haynes

Published by WorldChangers Media
PO Box 83, Foster, RI 02825
www.WorldChangers.Media

This book is dedicated to all the women who came before us—the trailblazers, the activists, the scientists, the teachers, the healers, the mothers, the grandmothers, the wise women, and all the women who have created changes both big and small in their families, communities, and workplaces.

Standing on your shoulders, we can change the world.
Thank you.

Table of Contents

WHEN WOMEN ARE WELL, EVERYONE WINS

"I'm interested in women's health because I'm a woman. I'd be a darn fool not to be on my own side."

- MAYA ANGELOU

Introduction

ANCA GRIFFITHS

For women, health is the ultimate glass ceiling. And yet, as with so many other barriers to life, liberty, and equality, those affected by it don't always see it clearly until they are pressed against its edge.

The challenges women face around their health are so commonplace, and so universally experienced, that many women don't even realize they are at play.

Over the last several years, I have spoken with tens of thousands of women around the globe regarding women's health topics—including internationally-recognized medical experts, holistic and traditional providers, and professional women climbing the corporate ladder. One of the most common responses I get from women outside the medical field is, "I can't see how this applies to me. I'm fine. Why are we even talking about this?" And yet, when asked, many of these same women report chronic issues like anxiety, depression, insomnia, painful menstruation, inflammation, and autoimmune concerns.

Are these women "sick" by conventional definition? Maybe not. But neither are they operating at optimal levels of health. In fact, they're so conditioned to expect a sub-par experience around health that they can't see the truth—that being a woman doesn't have to mean accepting pain, suffering, or limitations. More, they don't realize that a large part of their suffering is because their healthcare options are not designed for them—and, in some cases, may actually be taking advantage of them.

Women who know women

Having lived, worked, and taught in multiple locations on three continents over the last twenty years, I can confidently say that the need for better information, education, and support around women's health is universal. Different cultures and disciplines have different strengths and challenges around women's health; one of the gifts of a global information system is that we can learn from them all.

While I routinely present to audiences in the thousands about how women can start winning at health, I am not a doctor or health provider. Like many of you reading this book, I am simply a woman who, when confronted with medical challenges that showed me the limits of my self-sufficiency, realized that something was missing. During one of the most vulnerable times in my life, I had nowhere to turn to find the resources I needed to make confident decisions about my health. When I looked for credible experts in the online space, there were few to be found.

I'll share much more about my personal journey throughout this book, but one key moment in my quest to find the best women's health experts was when I read *Sex Matters: How Male-Centric Medicine Endangers Women's Health, and What We Can Do About It*, by Alyson J. McGregor, MD, who is among the most recognized sex and gender medicine experts in the world.

That book opened my eyes even further to the need for women, as consumers of healthcare, to have access to accurate, actionable information and advocate for themselves within the healthcare system. Intrigued, I reached out to Dr. McGregor to share my intentions around creating a platform of highly-qualified experts to support women around the globe to create optimal health.

To my immense joy, Dr. McGregor was intrigued, and introduced me to our third cofounding partner, Dr. Marjorie Jenkins, MD, who serves as the Dean of the University of South Carolina School of Medicine Greenville and Chief Academic Officer for Prisma Health - Upstate. Like Dr. McGregor, Dr. Jenkins is passionate about improving outcomes and experiences for women across all sectors of health, and has been tireless in advocating for research, representation, and education of women within the medical world.

"The only way to create meaningful change," Dr. McGregor said to me during one of our conversations, "is for women to fully understand their bodies and be able to advocate for themselves and their health with their providers. Anca, if you can create that awareness, and equip women with the tools they need to navigate real-life health situations, it will accelerate all of the changes we're already fighting for inside the system. Your work is the other half of the equation."

"So, let's do this together!" I replied.

The result of our partnership is our precision health platform, OM, where we provide a place for global health experts to connect directly with the women who will benefit from their knowledge, wisdom, and experience. In this book, as we do in our online spaces, we will share multiple personal and clinical perspectives to support you in understanding the health-related challenges facing women everywhere, and equip you with the knowledge and tools to actually do something about it. The information and research you'll find on these pages isn't a product of my own investigations, but rather comes directly from Dr. McGregor's and Dr. Jenkins's groundbreaking research and vast clinical experience as well as the research and experience of other renowned experts. Together, we are women who know women—and together, we stand for women's right to make informed and aligned decisions about all areas of their personal wellbeing.

When we imagine women "winning" at health, we see a future where women have direct access to experts who are on the cutting edge of clinical research and specialized practice. Instead of the multi-year lag that now exists between research breakthroughs and widespread implementation in medical protocols, we are creating direct-to-consumer pathways that empower women to learn what's working *now*, and understand the full spectrum of options around their health goals and challenges.

Who this book is for

This book is a conversation about health for women who are already having a conversation about health—and also for women who may not yet know they need to have a conversation about health.

6

This book is a broad overview of the challenges women face across the broad spectrum of "health"—including medical experiences, wellness practices, mental and emotional health, and more. Our intention is to present the massive scope of the issue in a way that will benefit as many people as possible. I think of it as "the 30,000-foot view." The barriers to optimal health you will learn about in this book literally touch every woman on this planet, as well as those who love and depend on them.

In this work, we will explore many possible avenues of health and healthcare—including conventional Western medicine, ancient traditions like Traditional Chinese Medicine and Ayurveda, and other proven health practices. Since our topics cover a wide range of healthcare approaches, we have chosen to use the blanket term "healthcare providers" or simply "providers" to refer to all of the doctors, physicians, specialists, mental health experts, nutritionists, practitioners of alternative and complementary therapies, and other credentialed experts who may be assisting you on your healthcare journey.

In the context of this book, we are defining "women" as people born with female biology—meaning, an XX chromosomal profile. For the purposes of this discussion, it's important to understand that while sex is biological, gender is a spectrum. The health and medical information we share in this book is based on a solidly-researched foundation of sex differentiation in the presentation of disease, pain, neurology, and many other factors. Therefore, we believe that, regardless of gender expression, all readers who have female biological markers and/or lived experiences as women will find the contents of this book to be of value in their personal health journey.

We understand and acknowledge that there are unique, pressing, and even life-threatening issues facing many groups within the broader collective of "women"—including, but not limited to, people of color, gay people, transgender people, and nonbinary people. While we cannot, within the limited scope of this particular book, conduct a full and nuanced exploration of these issues, our experts *are* having these vital conversations on the OM platform, and we are always open to hearing about and learning from your unique health experience. If you have a story of your own to share, start a conversation with us at contact@om-experts.com.

You are not alone

If you're wondering what you can do to create optimal health for yourself as a woman, or if you are struggling to connect with the resources and support you need to win in your own healthcare journey, you are not alone. Our mission is to empower you, and women everywhere, with the resources and support you need to change the narrative and thrive beyond the current status quo. This book is intended to dismantle our personal, cultural, and systemic misconceptions around what "health" actually means for women and those who identify as women.

My hope—and the hope of my expert coauthors and contributors—is that, by the time you turn the last page, you will understand the key challenges of the current healthcare paradigm, shift any conditioned resistance to creating your own optimal health journey, and feel empowered to seek the support you need so that you *can* win at health in whatever way is most meaningful for you—because when women are well, everyone wins.

WE DIDN'T WRITE THE RULES, BUT WE CAN CHANGE THEM

"A woman's health is her capital."
- HARRIET BEECHER STOWE

CHAPTER ONE

Hitting the Glass Ceiling

ANCA GRIFFITHS

"You really don't give a damn about your job anymore."

Chloe, one of my Parisian colleagues, had come to Hong Kong for a series of meetings. We were seated in an impressive conference room in the global headquarters of the luxury brand management company for which we worked. From my seat, I had a beautiful view of the Hong Kong harbor—and before Chloe's words jolted me out of my trance, I'd been staring at the sunlight as it danced along the water.

Chloe made her comment with a bit of a laugh, and in French (so most of the people in the room wouldn't understand), but it hit me hard all the same. Throughout that day's session, I had maintained an aloof silence, without offering much of an opinion—a stark difference from my usual enthusiasm. I had hoped I could finish the meeting without anyone calling me out, but obviously I'd been mistaken.

I loved my job from day one. Ten years in, I still had no desire to do anything else. My team had become like a family. And yet, in that moment, I could not have cared less about the matter at hand.

You see, less than a week before, I'd suffered a miscarriage. I'd only been ten weeks along. Aside from my husband, Evan, no one—not even my parents—knew I'd been pregnant. I had no idea what to do, or how to feel. The whole experience had been so bewildering that I could not even cry. So, I just kept showing up, shoved everything I was feeling down as deep as I could, and tried to adjust my demeanor.

Thankfully, everyone filed out of the meeting shortly thereafter, and I was able to snatch a few minutes alone in the women's toilet. I looked myself in the mirror and saw that, despite heavy makeup and a genuine attempt to put myself together, I looked ... blah. I felt tired, numb, and deeply sad.

Until that day, I never considered health to be a major factor in my career. I was in my early thirties and had few physical struggles. Even my menstrual cycles involved little in the way of pain or emotional shifts. I was careful about my nutrition, exercised, and integrated the latest "superpower" ingredients—like turmeric, green tea, and chia seeds—that came up regularly in the social media accounts I followed. I thought I had my health under control.

Now, I felt for the first time that my body was broken. It was getting in the way of my desire to be a mother and inhibiting my performance at work. However, this wasn't the flu; I couldn't simply tell everyone I was sick and stay home for a few days. Calling in sick for a miscarriage just wasn't done. Besides, my OB-GYN said I was fine—that the miscarriage had been "clean," and that "this happens quite often. It's normal."

So, despite the fact that I felt physically and emotionally unfit to work, there I was, sitting in that conference room like nothing had happened.

Chloe's comment shook me. It intensified the feeling that I was losing control of my body. It bothered me enough that I started looking for help. After all, I had "Doctor Google" at my fingertips; surely there was information and support available for women in my position?

I discovered that, worldwide, around one in four pregnancies end in miscarriage. That shocked me. There were hundreds of women in my office building alone. How could it be possible that I'd never heard about this happening to any of them? More, the information available to me online seemed to be limited to a few bullet-pointed articles on WebMD and a few back-corner forums that gave women a space to vent their feelings, but offered very little practical information for healing.

How was it possible that there are hundreds of websites devoted to solving the trivial problem of cellulite and "crepey skin," but so little support for a real health matter like miscarriage? Despite having literally a world of knowledge at my fingertips, I was back to feeling adrift, alone, and unsupported.

My eyes were opened through that experience. The stats showed that I was not the only woman going through this, so why the silence on the matter from the health and wellness community? Why was my experience of pregnancy loss brushed off, minimized, or flat-out ignored by my healthcare providers? Why was I expected to pretend that something so traumatic to both my body and my psyche *did not happen*?

Why was *no one* talking about this?

None of this made sense to me as a woman. Nor did it make sense to me from a business perspective. Businesses—including healthcare companies—exist to solve problems. A large part of my job in the luxury market was around identifying opportunities for our brands to fill a gap. This was, quite honestly, the biggest gap I'd ever encountered. It was like one plus one plus one equaled zero.

And then, it hit me: If I—an otherwise healthy, well-edu-cated, financially secure woman living in a country with one of the most robust medical systems on the planet—was experienc-ing this massive gap in support around something as common as pregnancy loss, what were other women contending with? What were *they* keeping silent about?

Why aren't women winning at health?

The more I turned my attention to the market of women's health, the more shocked I was by the reality I discovered.

By applying my decades of knowledge about market analysis and behavioral trends among consumer populations, connecting with global experts in both Western medicine and traditional modalities, researching trends within the health and wellness community, and eventually creating a global platform to support and educate women to be informed consumers of health, I began to discover the *real* reasons why the help I needed after my mis-carriage wasn't available to me when I needed it.

The information you're about to discover isn't likely to turn up during your standard Google search. In fact, I only became privy to much of what you'll discover in this book *after* I built a platform to bring together the best minds in women's health from around the globe—including my amazing coauthors, Dr. Jenkins and Dr. McGregor. The media certainly isn't featuring this information. The wellness websites aren't pumping out this content every hour. Most general practitioners and OB-GYNs aren't sharing it; in fact, unless they've made women's health outcomes an area of specialty, they likely don't know it exists.

Together, my coauthors and I have done something few, if any, have attempted before: to analyze the true scope and depth of the problems around women's health, and begin to plant the seeds of a solution.

As you'll see in a moment, there are four key factors impacting women's health today. Each of these factors seems independent, but in fact strengthens and exerts an influence upon the others; this keeps women locked in a cycle of misinformation, frustration, and lack of support. Some you may have personal experience with; others, you may never have considered. All will be explored in detail throughout this book, with the aim of empowering you to become an informed consumer of health and healthcare, for both yourself and the women who matter to you.

The four key factors that prevent women from winning at health are:

1. The global male-centric medical system
2. The predatory wellness industry
3. The minimization and discreditation of traditional health practices

4. Women's internalized behaviors, beliefs, and
   assumptions about their health and wellbeing.

The fourth and final factor was what triggered my realization
after Chloe's comment that day in the conference room and sent
me down the "rabbit hole" of research and analysis. My struggle
wasn't caused just by my miscarriage itself, but also by my belief—
reinforced by our work culture and society at large—that my miscarriage was shameful and shouldn't be talked about.

The more I learned about the first three factors impacting
women's health, the more I realized that the greater outcome,
ultimately, hinges on us as individuals. If women want to win at
health, we need to find better, more meaningful solutions together
through information, education, and honest communication. On
some level, you know this too, because you picked up this book.

The science and stories I and my coauthors share in the
coming chapters may shock, anger, and frustrate you. You may
feel, as I did, that nearly everything you've previously learned
about health and wellness is wrong. You may get the sense that
the entire system is broken—and, in many ways, it is. Yet, our goal
is not simply to share what's wrong, but also to reveal the amazing
miracle that is the female body and present a path to reclaim the
narrative around our health for the benefit of all.

If we, as women, could learn to relate differently to our health
without shame, guilt, or fear; educate ourselves about our female
biology beyond the areas of reproductive health and "bikini
medicine"; and, most of all, speak out about our health to our
healthcare providers and to one another, all of the other factors
that impact women's health would begin to change in response.
They would have no choice but to change.

How do I know this? Because I understand *markets*.

In any given market situation, there are really only two players: the market itself (meaning, the businesses involved and those who produce for and support those businesses), and consumers. The market for women's health is comprised of two main parts: the traditional (Western) medical system of hospitals and providers, and the "wellness" system that lives mostly online. The consumers for this market are, of course, women themselves.

However, unlike literally any other market on the planet, the health market is *not* optimized to serve its customers. In fact, it doesn't appear to consider them much at all. Despite women making *80 percent of consumer decisions* with regard to health services and products, women's needs are routinely minimized, or even outright ignored.

This dynamic of "market dissonance" is both created and underpinned by the four factors I shared above.

First, there's the male-centric medical system. As we'll explore further in chapters to come, almost nothing in our current medical system is developed for women. From our understanding of disease, to diagnostic procedures, to hospital protocols, to pharmaceuticals, to diet, to exercise ... all of it was designed for and studied in men, and then retroactively applied to women. Anything to do with womanhood and female bodies—especially key physiological transition points like menstruation, childbearing, perimenopause, and menopause—is treated as an addendum in the body of medical knowledge. As if to say, "Oh, those are just the extra things women do."

This wouldn't be a problem if the things that work for men worked for us, too—but they don't. This shows in the numbers. Globally, women live longer than men but do so in worse health, spending up to 15 percent of their lives coping with disease (as compared to 12 percent for men).[1] A recent Danish study found an enormous gender gap in diagnosis times, with women on average being diagnosed four years later than men across all types of disease.[2] Heart disease is the number one killer of both men and women in the United States, but women suffering from cardiac events are 50 percent more likely to be misdiagnosed,[3] and up to 70 percent more likely to die.

And that's just the tip of the iceberg. As you'll learn in Chapter Two, across all aspects of research, diagnosis, treatment, and education, our male-centric medical systems treats women as "atypical" men, rather than biologically unique beings—which results in suboptimal outcomes for most women and hundreds of thousands of unnecessary deaths each year for women around the world.

Given this glaring disparity, wouldn't it make sense—even from a purely financial perspective—for the health market to create an adapted product for women? However, while experts like my coauthors Dr. Jenkins and Dr. McGregor are working tirelessly toward that end, and much progress has been made in the last decade, change is painfully slow.

With women suffering disproportionately in the medical system, the online wellness industry has attempted to step in and solve some of the most visible issues. However, the focus of the wellness industry is almost totally vanity-based. It preys on women's fears around getting old, gaining weight, or being unattractive, because these fears sell products. Sometimes, the buzzwords of the moment (like *mindfulness, stress,* or *relaxation*) get sprinkled in, but unlike the men's wellness industry—which is based on performance, enhancement, and solving critical issues— women's wellness is all about "fixing."

Much of the science behind wellness products comes directly from the male-centric medical system. Despite the fact that the overwhelming majority of their audience is female, wellness industries pull data from studies and research conducted by, and for, men, on male subjects, and according to male parameters. Everything from weight loss to sleep to athletic performance is designed to work for men, and then marketed to women. Then, when these remedies inevitably fail to work with our unique biology, women blame themselves and go looking for another "cure."

Traditional, holistic methods of supporting health and wellness—including Traditional Chinese Medicine (TCM), Ayurveda, and Western herbalism—have been sidelined and discredited by both the medical system and the wellness industry. In the medical world, these sciences have been stripped of their gravitas and, until recently, were dismissed as "primitive" and unworthy of research. In wellness, they've become buzzwords and marketing tools—like, "Discover the ancient Chinese secret to beautiful hair!" In both cases, the power of traditional practices to support women's bodies in all stages of life has been diminished, and much of the wisdom of our foremothers has been lost.

So, in the midst of all this, is it any wonder that women are confused about how to win at health? That we suffer in silence, alone, while blaming ourselves or feeling guilty that neither medicine nor wellness products work for us? That we still, despite all our global advancements, can't easily access basic information about our most prevalent health challenges?

And yet, there is still one more facet to the problem—and that lies not outside us, but within us. We have been conditioned to expect less than optimal outcomes for ourselves across all areas of health, simply because ... we are women.

To understand how this happens, you must first understand that 95 percent of the brain's activity is unconscious; the vast majority of the decisions we make, the actions we take, and the emotions we feel play out beyond our conscious awareness. These subconscious drivers include habits and patterns, automatic body function, creativity, emotions, personality, beliefs, values, cognitive biases, and long-term memory.

Now, consider that, for thousands of years, we have been taught that women's bodies and minds are inherently "less than." That, as the "weaker sex," our very biology makes us irrational, weak, and hysterical. All of us, without exception, have been educated by our families, our cultures, our environments, and the world at large about the nuances of womanhood. Regardless of how far we've come in the last century, these old beliefs still impact how we relate to ourselves, our health, and each other on both an individual and a global level. And while, in the last fifty years or so, we've done a great job of addressing the obvious aspects of inequality for women, much of the subtext remains ingrained.

As Kaouthar Darmoni said in her groundbreaking TEDx talk, "We feminists have become detached from our feminine lineage ... in doing so, the unique value of the feminine has been sacrificed. Women's emancipation became women's masculinization."

With so few positive associations around womanhood, how can we value and create equality around women's health? How can we, as women, finally make our unique health experiences important enough to prioritize, talk about, and create services around?

If this seems melodramatic, consider this. How many times have you heard menstruation, postpartum, perimenopause, or menopause discussed in a positive light? How often have you heard other women express gratitude for their menstrual cycles, except on the heels of a pregnancy scare? How many times have you seen a woman own her age with pride rather than embarrassment? How many times have you heard a woman speak positively about her overall experience as a woman, particularly when it comes to health and healthcare?

If you can't think of a single example, you're not alone. Nearly every woman I've spoken to, including women's health experts, has the same internalized biases and negative associations. I'm still working on them within myself.

Somewhere along the way, we were convinced that being a woman is a problem to be fixed, not a gift to be embraced. That the very things that make us women are, in fact, hurdles to success in our lives and careers. That we are biologically broken—and that in order to thrive, we must become something other than who we are.

If we, as women, want to win at health, we need to begin by challenging our individual and collective beliefs about what it means to be a woman—not only with rhetoric, but with evidence. More, we need to reclaim the narrative around our health, and reshape it in a way that supports us to thrive.

DR. MARJORIE JENKINS

It seems obvious to say that women experience better outcomes in all areas of life when they are in optimal health. Yet, the extent to which women are suffering is staggering.

As a sex and gender medicine expert who has served in a number of national leadership roles, I can confidently assert that there is no such thing as "gender-blind" medicine. For most of my career, I've been focused on the intersection of medicine and women's lived experiences. I have thousands of stories about women who have suffered as a result of ingrained misogyny and male-centric practices in our medical systems. However, it was a recent personal experience that really drove home for me how we, as women, see and prioritize our health.

A colleague of mine, a respected female specialist with a thriving practice, recently visited my home. Over dinner, she explained that she was having some health challenges. "I'm exhausted all the time, but I can't seem to get good sleep," she told me. "I'm gaining weight even though I eat better than I ever have, and I'm starting to experience atypical heart palpitations. I can't tell if it's anxiety or something else."

"Have you been to see your primary care doctor?" I asked.

"I don't have time. I'm too busy taking care of my own patients. Besides, I had a full workup done four months ago, and the tests showed nothing wrong."

I looked at her over my wine glass. "If you're not feeling well, there's something wrong. Let's talk it through. I can't support you in an official capacity because I'm not your doctor, but I can help you make a plan so you don't feel like your visit is a waste of time."

It quickly became clear that my colleague was in a stress spiral. Due to her workload and concerns about her patients, she hadn't been sleeping well. When deprived of good rest, cortisol levels become elevated. This can lead to feelings of anxiety, as well as strong cravings for sugar and starchy foods (the fuel the body needs to combat exhaustion). This leads to weight gain and gut imbalances, which can then lead to depression.

I see this pattern in women all the time. To help women heal, we need to break the cycle—either by regulating their sleep or balancing their hormones. Once one factor is reset, the downward spiral can reverse itself.

It was concerning that my colleague, as a female physician, didn't fully understand the cycle playing out in her own body— but then, why would she? Without a specialization in sex and gender medicine, she might never have encountered research about how women's bodies deal with stress. Sadly, such information still isn't considered "mainstream" in the medical world. But that wasn't why this encounter stood out to me.

My colleague, despite being educated at the highest level and succeeding in a field that is dominated by men, was still operating on the uniquely female assumption that *she must take care of others at all costs.* In her, I saw the ongoing battle between what society expects of women and what women want for themselves. When her male colleagues felt less than optimally well, it wasn't an issue for them to visit their own doctors—so why was it so hard for her to prioritize her own wellbeing?

In the end, I got her to agree to make an appointment with her primary care provider, suggested some key tests to make sure she wasn't suffering from adrenal fatigue or common nutritional deficiencies, and recommended that she ask for a prescription sleep aid. However, in order to coax that agreement from her, I had to remind her that she couldn't provide the best care for her patients if she herself was unwell. What she wasn't willing to do for herself, she would do for her patients.

We, as women, face many obstacles in our fight for equality in the medical field. As both a patient and a provider, my passion is to do all I can in my lifetime to reverse the patterns in medicine that undermine women's health and wellbeing—whether those come from within the medical establishment or from within us as individuals.

After decades of study and clinical experience, I can unequivocally say that the biggest force for change when it comes to women's health is women's voices.

Every problem we have—clinically and otherwise—is compounded when we don't talk about it. Women and people with female biology have unique needs that our current systems simply do not account for. In part, this is a failure of the systems themselves, but it's also a failure of communication—and those failures in combination result in suboptimal health outcomes for millions of women every year. Therefore, changing the conversation around women's health isn't a matter of convenience. It's literally a matter of life and death.

We didn't write the rules, but we can change them.

MALE CENTRICITY KEEPS WOMEN FROM WINNING AT HEALTH

"Communities and countries, and
ultimately the world, are only as strong
as the health of their women."
- MICHELLE OBAMA

CHAPTER TWO

Modern Medicine is Male-Centric Medicine

DR. ALYSON MCGREGOR

When I began my career in medicine, I told people that my focus was "women's health." The inevitable response was, "Oh, you're a gynecologist!"

Well, no.

What I didn't realize, as a newly-certified emergency medicine physician, was that, to the greater medical community, "women's health" did not refer to the overall health and wellbeing of women. Rather, it was a term equivalent to what we've since nicknamed "bikini medicine"—meaning, care focused on women's reproductive organs.

How can "women's health" not refer to the health of the whole woman? I wondered. Aren't we more than just our breasts, uteri, and ovaries? Isn't there more to being a woman than the things that make us ... not men?

Those questions sent me on a journey to uncover why women are not treated as whole beings within our medical systems. What I found was a pattern of excluding, minimizing, and sidelining women that reaches all the way back to the roots of modern medicine. Our medical models, from clinical practice to research and education, are inherently male-centric. In every way, they are created to serve, study, and evaluate men—and women are suffering as a result.

Today, I'm an internationally-recognized expert in the field of sex and gender medicine and the cofounder of the Sex and Gender Women's Health Collaborative. Along the way, I have connected and collaborated with incredible women in the medical field—including our coauthor, Dr. Jenkins—to change the way all aspects of medicine are practiced, researched, and taught.

As you'll learn in this chapter, women are biologically different from men in every way: physically, emotionally, neurologically, and socially. Every cell in our body contains sex chromosomes which influence not only the growth and development of reproductive organs, but also digestion and metabolism, brain function and memory, the way we perceive and process pain, and more. We need care that honors our unique bodies and experiences—and yet, for the most part, we are not receiving it, because *our entire medical system is inherently male-centric.*

How did we get here?

In order to understand how and why our modern medical system is male-centric, we need to examine its roots.

Before the evolution of the modern scientific model, medicine in the West was based on the Hippocratic tradition and studied the movement and balance of the four "humors" (blood, yellow bile, black bile, and phlegm) and four elements (earth, fire, water and air) within the body. While there were medical schools in existence throughout Europe—most notably the school in Salerno, Italy—doctors mostly served the wealthy nobility. For rural and working-class society, women were the primary healers. They were herbalists, midwives, and caregivers to the sick, and operated within traditions passed down through many generations from woman to woman. Often, these traditions were a mystery to men, and women who were too successful at healing with them were branded "witches."

During the Enlightenment, the study of anatomy and the development of more robust clinical research models sparked the next phase of Western medicine's evolution. As the practice of dissection became widespread, much of the wisdom from previous medical models was questioned and even repudiated.

But here's where it gets interesting.

The practice of dissection and the science of anatomy made a huge contribution to the medical world. Knowledge about the inner workings of the human body expanded rapidly, and major contributions were made to the field as a result. However, nearly all of the bodies available to the medical schools were male. Religious beliefs at the time cautioned "upstanding" people against donating their bodies to research, so most of the available cadavers were hanged criminals and other societal outcasts—again, most of whom were male. In fact, archaeological excavation of hospital cemeteries in both the U.S. and U.K. have shown that, on average, at least three times as many men as women were dissected as part of early medical research. Without modern technologies and testing to support their observations, it was easy for these early research teams to conclude that the only differences between men and women were their sexual organs—after all, everyone, regardless of sex, has a heart, kidneys, lungs, bones, and skin.

Today, we know that the functions of many organs and systems are influenced by biological sex, and that sex hormones play a role in everything from digestion to how we perceive pain. However, that early male-centric research formed the basis for all of our subsequent discoveries, and led to a series of faulty assumptions around how women's bodies are, and are not, different from men's.

I want to note here that, while I'm centering this discussion on Western medicine as the origin of our current global care systems, there are many other medical systems originating in other parts of the world. In China, the system now known as Traditional Chinese Medicine (TCM) has been in practice for at least 2,200 years. In India, Ayurveda has been practiced as a formalized medicine system, including specialized schools, since as early as the third century B.C. As these were likely not well known to the founders of modern Western medicine and so had less influence on initial research models, I'm omitting them from this part of our discussion. However, as we'll explore later in this book, these wise and nuanced systems were later overridden by the global spread of the Western male-centric medical model, ultimately to the detriment of women.

As Western medicine evolved, women's challenges, both

physical and emotional, were sidelined by the ongoing assumption that their bodies were fundamentally the same as men's. Not only were women studied mostly in terms of the elements that made them "not male"—i.e., their sex organs—but they were also largely barred from the halls of medical institutions. Until quite recently, female perspectives were rarely, if ever, included in discussions of disease expression, treatment, or patient experience. Religious and cultural beliefs that women were "created from" men or genetically inferior to men permeated even the most rigorous science in the earlier parts of the twentieth century. Women were, over and over, reduced to the sum of their parts.

This dynamic has begun to change in the last few decades, as both our observational capabilities and women's presence in all areas of medical practice have increased, but we still have a long way to go.

Research which has been proven according to accepted scientific methods is rarely questioned; instead, it forms the bedrock upon which all other research rests. However, most, if not all, of our foundational research has been produced using male subjects and from a male perspective. Clinical trials are overwhelmingly designed to male standards using male animals—in part, to offset the complications of pregnancy testing and hormonal fluctuations in female participants. Studies which center male diseases or concerns are more likely to be funded. And, while we've seen an uptick in female participation in drug trials recently, only a small percentage of those studies actually account for sex differences in the data. As a result, the majority of FDA drug recalls have been due to "unforeseen" side effects in women.[1], [2]

In clinical practice, male centricity means that we don't fully understand how women experience disease. New research is revealing that female presentations of common conditions like heart disease and stroke don't resemble established male models or symptoms at all. Issues that primarily affect women, such as autoimmune diseases, menopause, uterine diseases, and chronic pain, are some of the most understudied in the medical world. Our lack of understanding affects outcomes for women across the globe, every day. And yet, when women say, "There's something wrong," we don't believe them.

In this chapter, I'll share with you four key areas of health where male-centric medicine is endangering women: heart health, brain health, pharmaceuticals, and pain. While this is by no means an exhaustive discussion, my intention is to help you understand exactly how pervasive male centricity is within our medical structures, and how it keeps women from winning at health. Once you see it, you will no longer be able to ignore it.

Women experience disease differently

Heart disease is the number one killer of women around the world. And yet, when women come into the emergency department having a heart attack, their symptoms often go unrecognized. In fact, women are *highly unlikely* to fit the textbook model of a heart attack—meaning, the acute chest pain and left arm pain that we see so often in TV hospital dramas. Instead, they are more likely to feel diffuse pressure in the chest, shortness of breath, fatigue, jaw and neck pain, and "brain fog," sometimes for days or weeks before the actual cardiac event. Disturbingly, women themselves may not even recognize that they are having a heart attack, because they too have been taught to look for the classic male symptoms! They simply know that something is wrong.

The result is that women are up to *three times more likely* to die after a serious heart attack than men. Of those who do die, a 2016 study found, nearly half had no previous diagnosis of heart disease[3]—or, more accurately, exhibited no previous symptoms consistent with male models of heart disease, and so received no conclusive diagnosis.

You see, women's heart disease often manifests as diffuse inflammation in the system of smaller blood vessels, rather than the larger "blocked arteries" we most often hear about in men. This is known as "microvascular disease" and is closely linked to inflammation. When inflammation narrows the blood vessels around the heart, it results in stress to the heart muscle, which can, if left untreated, trigger a major coronary event (aka, a heart attack).

Microvascular disease, which falls under the category of "ischemic heart disease," is far more common in women than obstructive coronary artery disease.[4] Yet, in medical literature, female presentation of heart conditions is still described as "atypical." Because our models identify male patterns of heart disease as "typical," all of our tests and diagnostic procedures (such as echocardiograms, angiograms, and stress tests) are designed to identify those symptoms. Our pharmaceutical treatment options—such as antihypertensives and cholesterol-lowering drugs—are likewise focused on treating male symptoms in male bodies and may have little to no effect on predominantly female heart disease types.

While well-known factors like high cholesterol, high triglycerides, and high blood pressure are indicators for heart disease in women as well as men, we are only just beginning to understand how other factors—like hormonal fluctuations, mental health, and inflammation—contribute to heart-related conditions. For example, new studies have uncovered a link between heart disease and pregnancy-related complications like preeclampsia, eclampsia, and gestational diabetes. A 2016 study by Brigham Health showed that women under forty who suffered from endometriosis were *three times more likely* to develop heart disease and arterial blockages than other women in the same age group due to increased systemic inflammation.[5] Given that it currently takes an average of nine years for a woman to get a diagnosis of endometriosis (in part because, like so many other diseases specific to women, we haven't studied it well), and that women under forty are not considered statistically susceptible to heart attacks under our current models, this is a massive issue. When these women do seek treatment for their female-specific heart disease symptoms, they are far more likely to be diagnosed with some other condition—most frequently, anxiety—and sent home with instructions to "calm down and take it easy."

In fact, across the board, anxiety is the most common misdiagnosis for women suffering from female-specific heart disease. Anxiety is the most commonly diagnosed mental health condition overall and is nearly twice as common among women as men.[6] However, as more research emerges around female pattern heart disease, we are observing a high correlation between heart attack symptoms and the physical symptoms of anxiety. Severe panic attacks and female-pattern coronary events look disturbingly similar at first glance. Because doctors and hospital staff are trained to look for male-pattern coronary symptoms, many women who are actually having cardiac events are treated as mental health patients and never receive any screening for heart disease at all. We have no idea how many women die as a direct result of this—but we do know that their final medical records will likely say, "Exhibited no previous symptoms."

This is just a tiny glimpse into the ways in which male-centric medicine impacts women's heart health. There are near-infinite nuances within this subject, and the fact that we are beginning to unlock some of the secrets to women's heart health feels exciting. However, progress is not happening nearly fast enough. Most hospitals and care facilities have few, if any, protocols for screening women differently than men when they present with heart-related symptoms. We still don't have drugs or treatment protocols available to address inflammation as a primary cause of women's heart disease. Therefore, it's up to us as individuals to educate ourselves and insist on the care we deserve. Simply asking healthcare providers, "What criteria are you basing that diagnosis on?" is a great way to start a conversation. Also be aware that your health record is an important piece of real estate that *you* now own (especially since services like MyChart, which allow you to read your medical records in real time, have come into effect). If you think you might be dealing with a cardiovascular issue, say so—and make sure this information makes it into your chart. Most of all, don't discount your gut feelings—and if you don't feel like you're being heard, please get a second opinion.

Women's brains are different

Sex hormones are vital to the development of the entire central nervous system (CNS). Women's brains operate differently than men's in many ways, not the least of which is our physiological response to internal and external stressors.

Since neuroscience is not my area of specialty, I spoke to my colleague, Dr. Larry Cahill, Professor of Neurobiology and

Behavior at the University of California, Irvine. He's one of the world's foremost experts on how biological sex influences the human brain, particularly in the areas of emotion, memory, and behavior. Dr. Cahill says:

"Our brains are deeply sex-influenced. As you may have guessed, this has important implications all over the place in women's lives. There's a big gap between what we are learning and how that translates into clinical care—but we are making great strides toward integrating what we know into the daily reality of medical practice.

"One thing that women everywhere should know is that women are two to three times more likely to have stress-related disorders of various sorts than men. Given comparable experience (including traumatic experience), women are nearly three times more likely than men to develop anxiety or post-traumatic stress disorder (PTSD). This has to do with the way the brain develops during adolescence.

"When we as humans get excited, aroused, or fearful, a spot in the brain we call the *locus coeruleus* (literally, 'the blue place') activates, spreading norepinephrine, a stress hormone, throughout the brain and activating stress responses in the body. Before puberty, males and females (referring to biological sex, not gender identity) have similar reactivity to catalyzing events. However, during and after puberty, the activation of the *locus coeruleus* is ten times higher in females. Most likely, this is an adaptation that prepares the female body for motherhood by attuning her to threats to her offspring. However, in our modern life, this means that women are more responsive than men to perceived threats—including social/societal threats and threats around key personal relationships—which translates to higher levels of worry, anxiety, and stress-related illnesses."

To me, as a physician, this is actually encouraging information. We as women tend to be perceived as oversensitive, overreactive, or "hysterical," particularly in stressful situations like a hospital visit. In the medical literature, the greater activation of our *locus coeruleus* under stress is termed "hyperresponsive." However, we are only hyperresponsive when compared to a male baseline; while current protocols want to make women wrong for not fitting into the textbook guidelines, what is "normal" for women has not, in fact, been established.

Knowing that our brains are wired to be more sensitive to stimuli can help us understand why we feel "different" to our male colleagues and counterparts (particularly in stressful or tense situations), and why we experience burnout at higher rates.

Dr. Cahill went on to say:

"There is still much more to understand in terms of the neuroscience of sex influences and how these biological and functional differences impact women's everyday lives. The brain is such a complex organ. We're only beginning to scratch the surface in terms of 'fundamental' knowledge—meaning, knowledge of what is shared by and true for, all human beings regardless of sex, gender, race, or age. Sex influences add another layer of complexity. However, as we move toward a model of 'personalized medicine,' sex influences are some of the first and most basic things we'll need to consider. We can't skip over them. In fact, we can't personalize anything without addressing the impacts of biological sex and gonadal hormones, because those factors are present and integrated in every organ and system in the body."

If you are experiencing stress, anxiety, or other neurological or emotional symptoms, my advice is to *be* an advocate and *bring* an advocate. Unfortunately, women's mental health symptoms are still not treated with appropriate gravity in many health settings; having someone you trust with you can make it easier to communicate with your provider and make sure you get the help you need.

Drugs don't work the same for women

Biological sex determines far more than whether you grow a penis and testes or a uterus and ovaries. Sex chromosomes are present in every cell of our bodies and, combined with our hormonal profiles, influence everything about our physiological state.

One place where sex differences play a key role is metabolism. Women digest food, alcohol, and pharmaceuticals differently than men. The liver and kidneys are "sexed" organs, meaning they process food and medication differently depending on whether their chromosomal makeup is XX or XY, as well as the balance of hormones in the body; a recent study found over 1,000 sex-based differences in the livers of male and female animals! This means that women may require different doses, different dosing frequency, and even different drug formulations than men to get the same results—but again, we aren't sure what this looks like, because it hasn't been extensively studied.

As we noted earlier, women have historically experienced the majority of adverse drug events. In fact, just being female means your risk of having an adverse drug reaction is nearly twice as high; this likelihood only increases if you are on multiple medications. [7] In recent years (in large part due to the efforts of my colleague Dr. Jenkins and others), the number of recalls related to adverse drug reactions in women has shrunk dramatically—however, the problem is by no means resolved.

For example, the drug Labetalol, a commonly prescribed medication for high blood pressure, has no sex-related dosing recommendations, yet tests reveal up to 80 percent greater serum concentrations in women than in men. This "overdosing" can result in serious bleeding conditions, fainting, slowed heart rate, and even heart failure.[8] Daily aspirin, commonly recommended by doctors, does not in fact reduce women's risk of a first heart attack, and can be dangerous when used long-term because of the increased risk of bleeding disorders. Ibuprofen and other over-the-counter NSAID pain relievers have likewise been found to be less effective at relieving women's pain than men's, and come with a higher risk of adverse effects including liver injury. [9], [10]

Despite this emerging data, we're still essentially throwing drugs at women at the same dose approved for men and hoping for a benefit, because not enough has been done to integrate this new knowledge into health education and prescription guidelines. Many doctors today use computers or smartphone apps to look up medication dosing and frequency information when prescribing, but these databases have not been updated with sex-based recommendations.

However, clinical drug trials have, until recently, excluded women on the false assumption that menstrual and hormonal fluctuations impact overall trial results, and because women of childbearing age are considered "protected subjects" under the National Research Act of 1974. The Research Act itself was a response to the disastrous consequences of earlier, unregulated drug trials—in particular, that of Thalidomide, an anticonvulsive which was also marketed as a sleep aid and nausea reliever to pregnant women, and which caused over 10,000 babies to be born with severe birth defects. The measures taken to protect women of childbearing age from predatory drug companies had the unintended effect of erasing women from the clinical trial process almost entirely for over two decades.

While the numbers of women included in clinical trials has been steadily increasing over the last two decades, women often are not included until the third and final phase of the process—which means that, in some cases, the first time a new drug interacts with female cells is when it is nearly ready to go to market. In 2016, the National Institutes of Health (NIH) introduced a requirement that sex be part of cellular and animal studies as well—but, since not all research is funded by the NIH (and therefore subject to its guidelines), this is still not standard practice across all areas of research.

More, the ways in which trial data is separated and analyzed after the fact can make a huge difference in terms of outcomes for women. For example, if a trial's design does not include separating and analyzing data based on sex (instead of simply combining data from all participants into a single pool), many adverse effects for women can be hidden or minimized because they are offset by positive effects in male subjects—only to be discovered after the fact, when the drug is released to the public.

My coauthor Dr. Jenkins has worked closely with the FDA office that helped to create the FDA Drug Trial Snapshots—a guide for consumers that shows who was enrolled in drug trial studies by age, biological sex, gender, and race/ethnicity. There's still a notable lack of diversity—elderly women and women of color, the two groups most likely to have adverse drug reactions and interactions, are all but absent from most drug trials—and many times the results of women in a sample group register as "too small to calculate effectively," but it's slowly getting better.

As a woman, you can advocate for better pharmaceutical care by asking your healthcare providers to research sex-specific dosing and reactions for your prescriptions. Also, I recommend that every woman carry a list of all of her prescriptions in her wallet or phone; this helps your providers research possible interactions more effectively (and also update your digital medical records if necessary).

Finally, remember that you know your body better than anyone else. If you don't feel right after taking a new medication, or if you are experiencing adverse effects, don't just live with it. Say something—and if your provider doesn't believe you, get a second opinion.

Women feel pain differently

Outside of yearly physicals, most people seek medical care because they're in pain. However, in our current medical systems, women are less likely to receive adequate treatment for their pain, less likely to receive pain medication promptly and at appropriate dosages, and less likely to leave with a concrete diagnosis.

According to research, women have a lower pain tolerance and threshold than men for the same conditions. Since the only methods we have to evaluate pain rely on self-reporting, this is often used to minimize women's experiences.

However, there's more to this than women being "overly sensitive."

Women process pain differently than men. As we explored earlier, neurotransmission is sex differentiated; this includes pain responses. In fact, the parts of the brain that control the perception of pain have receptors for both estrogens and androgens. How pain is perceived is in part dependent on the levels and activity of these hormones in the body. (This is why pain of all kinds—including migraine and body aches—are more prevalent at certain points in the menstrual cycle.) More, researchers have found differences in gene expressions related to pain and inflammation between male and female subjects, indicating that women's bodies signal their brains differently when pain is perceived.

Women have much higher rates of pain disorders, many of which are tied directly to neurological and hormonal functions. One reason may be that pain receptors are influenced by estradiol levels, and so may be more or less sensitive depending on where a woman is in her cycle. Once a woman enters menopause and estrogen levels drop, all expressions of pain are exacerbated because decreased estrogens increase pain perception.

We know that these and many more sex differences exist with regard to pain, but we haven't studied them enough to fully understand them. In fact, a recent review in the medical journal,

Pain, noted that in the previous decade, 79 percent of pain studies included only male subjects, while only 8 percent were exclusively female, and only 4 percent studied sex differences![11] Instead, we throw drugs at the problem to see what sticks.

What does this mean for women?

First, if you have a pain condition, medications designed to suppress pain in men might not work as well, or at all, for you, or may vary in effect during the various phases of your menstrual cycle. Women are also more likely to experience unpleasant side effects from pain medication, particularly opioids, and achieve less consistent results because of the role of the menstrual cycle in pain perception.

Second, women are less likely to be believed when they express pain. Because research has shown women to be more sensitive to pain, our pain is minimized, brushed aside—or, worse, misdiagnosed as having a psycho-emotional origin. (Yes, some doctors really do think "it's all in your head.") Far too many women come into the emergency department with a pain complaint and leave without a specific diagnosis. She will likely then be referred to a psychologist or psychiatrist, who may diagnose her with a mental health issue like anxiety—or she may simply walk away thinking, "Am I imagining this?" This contributes to unnecessarily long diagnostic periods—as Anca shared in Chapter One, women on average need four years more than men to receive a diagnosis for *any* condition—as well as unnecessary suffering, loss of productivity, and diminished quality of life.

Finally, since women are more likely to experience pain flares at certain times of their cycle, they report inconsistent pain levels and results from treatment pathways. For healthcare providers who haven't been educated about sex differences in pain, this can translate as attention-seeking or "hysteria," and, if the woman asks for relief, may even be misconstrued as drug seeking. "But you weren't in this much pain a week ago" is a common response. Well, of course she wasn't. She was in a different phase of her cycle!

The more women speak up around their pain, it seems, the less they are believed. However, our inability to understand and manage women's pain is actually a direct failing of our male-centric medical system. The pervasive cultural belief that women are physically, intellectually, and emotionally inferior to men has made its way into our medical relationship with pain, and women are bearing the costs. Although both new research and evolving social norms are challenging these ideas, they are still ingrained in both medical education and in the attitudes of some individual providers.

Women want and deserve to be cared for and validated, not minimized and talked down to—especially when they are in pain. If you or someone you know is dealing with pain—whether acute or chronic—please seek out a healthcare provider who is willing to work with you toward a real solution. Ask direct questions and observe how your body feels and responds to pain at different points in your cycle. The more information you can share with your healthcare providers, the more likely you are to get appropriate care.

***

What we've explored in this chapter is only the tip of the iceberg in terms of the ways our male-centric medical system prevents women from winning at health. In the next chapter, Dr. Jenkins and I will explore how clinical practice overlaps with women's lived experiences in the medical system, and how we as women can take steps to create better care situations for ourselves and those we love.

WHEN WOMEN DON'T CHALLENGE THE STATUS QUO, ALL WOMEN PAY THE PRICE

"Real change, enduring change, happens one step at a time."

- RUTH BADER GINSBURG

CHAPTER THREE

Medicine, Mindset, and Money

DR. MARJORIE JENKINS

I was born and raised in Appalachia. The expectation in my region is that women will get married and have children young. Teenage marriage is common and widely accepted, and it's normal to see people becoming grandparents in their thirties. My sisters had babies in their teens. In my hometown, I'm an anomaly: I've been branded "the career woman." Sometimes this is said with respect; sometimes, with derision.

When I had my primary care practice, 75 percent of my patients were women. Hormonal challenges, menopause concerns, and other female concerns were a specialty.

However, when I became pregnant with my third child, I hid my pregnancy from patients as long as I could. I didn't want them to get nervous that I would no longer be there to take care of them. I assured everyone that I'd be back as soon as possible after the birth. My husband was a stay-at-home dad at the time, so I felt confident taking a shorter maternity leave.

What I wasn't expecting was the judgment I'd get around that choice. After my maternity leave, patients would often ask in a mildly accusing tone, "Where's the baby?" As if, by coming into the clinic to care for them, I was somehow neglecting my child. I got so tired of hearing that question that I started answering, in my best Appalachian drawl, "Oh, the baby? I left her in a nice dresser drawer. The dogs are keeping an eye on her."

Not everyone appreciated my humor.

As a woman, I was judged from all angles. By maintaining my career, I was perceived as failing in my duty to my family. On the flip side, by setting boundaries around seeing patients after 5:00 p.m. and on weekends, I was perceived as being on the "mommy track" by other physicians—meaning, less dedicated to the practice than my male or child-free counterparts.

The thing is, *I* was clear about who I was and what I wanted. *I* knew my children were happy and that my husband was a remarkable dad. As a family, we were doing fine. However, maintaining a balance amidst these layered expectations from others was a challenge. I struggled with guilt on a daily basis for much of my early career.

Women deal with multiple layers of expectations and biases every day. No matter how credentialed, successful, and accomplished, there are always parts of our lives that are under scrutiny and where we feel we are falling short. We are expected to be strong when in the boardroom and soft in the bedroom. We are expected to maintain a beautiful home while also maintaining our career. We are expected to take care of everyone else while minimizing our own needs for care and caring. In essence, we are expected to keep it all together while always putting ourselves last.

As the expectations—and the guilt—start stacking up, women can start to feel boxed in. We start making choices in service to these expectations rather than to our wellbeing. Many times, we only take the time to take care of ourselves when we are forced to—by disease, exhaustion, or outside circumstances.

Most of us have heard the phrase "the deck is stacked against you." For women, the "stacking" is mostly society's preconceived roles and behaviors, and the labeling of a woman based on gender. When cultural, religious, and familial expectations are added to the stack, it results in an even larger divide between the individual woman and her abilities to achieve optimal health and wellness. For example, in some cultures, being too thin is a sign that your husband isn't taking good care of you and your family; in these cultures, women's rates of obesity, diabetes, and heart disease are far above global averages. In some religious communities, talking about sex, menstruation, menopause, or anything else related to womanhood is either highly uncomfortable or outright taboo.

Every patient that engages with a healthcare provider brings into the room cultural and societal expectations along with their personal beliefs and values. These can contribute to a clinical visit which does not achieve what the woman needs. It can take the length of an appointment for some women to work up the courage to broach sensitive topics with their providers. When they finally do mention vaginal pain during sex, chronic tiredness, or disruptive hot flashes, the appointment is over and their provider is already halfway out the door. Instead of concern and empathy, they can be met with, "Let's make another appointment for you to come back so we can talk about this"—which means they'll be living with their symptoms for another three months or more, if they find the courage to come back at all.

In every culture and society, there's a list of things that "good" women don't do. Putting themselves first tops the list just about everywhere. When combined with the inherent challenges of a male-centric medical system, this dynamic makes it hard for women to get the care they need and deserve, because getting good care *requires* women to make themselves heard. Therefore, every woman should be encouraged to examine the many layers of beliefs and traditions that make it challenging for them to speak up about their health.

It is the responsibility of healthcare providers and the medical profession in general to evolve our protocols and diagnostic tools to not only reflect what we are learning about women's bodies and how they work, but also to create a safe space for women to be heard and listened to. If we do not achieve this, we will never begin to dismantle the "stack" and create truly personalized care.

Perception in practice

In addition to the internal "stacked" layers of expectations with which all women contend to some extent, there are external and intersectional factors that keep women from getting the care they need in our medical systems.

There is a pattern within our healthcare system to chop up women's experiences into clear chunks based on reproductive timelines. Clinical and research environments have developed a model of women's health "across the lifespan," which typically means parsing a woman into a particular category: pre-puberty, puberty, reproductive, post-reproductive, and geriatric stages. Once a woman has moved past a particular category, health professionals rarely ask about events or concerns which occurred in the past; however, this is not in the best interest of women. For example, the risk of heart disease in a woman's post-reproductive and geriatric years is powerfully influenced by her experience during pregnancy and postpartum, particularly if she suffered from gestational diabetes or preeclampsia. How many sixty-five-year-old women are asked about health issues that occurred during their pregnancies? In the same vein, when diagnosing menopausal women in their fifties, we rarely ask them about their menstrual symptoms during their twenties and thirties, yet the two are closely related. When we don't ask about a woman's full health history—including her reproductive experiences—we reduce her chances of receiving appropriate and timely diagnoses, screenings, and interventions which could be lifesaving.

In addition, there is conditioned tendency among older generations to "do what the doctor says." If the doctor says there's nothing wrong, there must be nothing wrong. Age-related factors like social isolation and cognitive decline combine to keep women agreeing with their providers, rather than starting productive conversations.

Then there are the challenges of racial, ethnic, and socioeconomic biases, which play out on both the individual and systemic levels. The single most underserved population group in the American medical system is Black, African American women. Hispanic women have only slightly better outcomes. Why?

BIPOC women are more likely to have high stress levels due to socioeconomic and cultural factors. They're more likely to have nutritional and preventive care challenges. And they're less likely to be heard by providers when they voice their complaints. Dr. Chinn et al published an article on this subject in the *Journal of Women's Health* in 2021. The following quote is so uniquely applicable in its clarity and eloquent in its conclusion that I include it here verbatim: "Health does not exist outside its social context. Without equity in social and economic conditions, health equity is unlikely to be achieved, and one cost of health inequality has been the lives of Black women."[1]

The complexities of the dynamics of perception, communication, and bias in the space of race and ethnicity are vast, and beyond the scope of this book. However, we are exploring them in depth on the OM platform and continuing to follow ongoing research.

"I believe you"

I've spent tens of thousands of hours in clinical situations with women of all ages, races, ethnicities, and backgrounds. Unequivocally, I have found that the three most powerful words I can say to a woman are, "I believe you."

Because our male-centric medical system isn't fully set up to diagnose and treat women's concerns, some women spend months or even years trying to get answers about their symptoms. When tests are "inconclusive," or their pain is nonspecific, or their specific issues aren't well-researched, women can easily slip into a "spin cycle" of provider visits and referrals with little to no positive outcome. I can't tell you how many of my female patients have been told, again and again, "We can't find anything wrong with you," even though they are obviously suffering.

If I let my mind go down the road of how many women are receiving substandard care right now, today, it can drive me to distraction. That's why my passion is to do all I can in the time I have to reverse this dynamic in medicine and create proactive, personalized care for everyone. While I do maintain that a medical education provides insight, context, and specialized skills that are invaluable to patient care, I also believe that *no one* knows a woman's body better than she herself does. We women have lived in our bodies since we were in utero. When something is wrong, we know it. We feel it. And when we express what we're feeling, we deserve to be heard.

In an ideal world, women would come to the table fully equipped to self-advocate and have productive conversations with their healthcare providers, and providers would have the time, bandwidth, and knowledge about women's unique bodies to listen, and to act upon that listening. However, as Dr. McGregor shared in Chapter Two, the medical community is only now coming to grips with the vast gaps in our knowledge around women's bodies, health, and lived experiences. It has taken decades of work in an attempt to ensure new research findings are taught to the next generations of healthcare providers. While change is happening, it's slow. This is why I believe in equipping women with the tools to become active in their own healthcare experience.

ANCA GRIFFITHS

I've lived and worked in multiple countries across three continents, and I've observed that female health is viewed differently in different locations.

"Hygiene de vie"

In the United States, Canada, and Asia, gynecological checkups are treated as an uncomfortable chore. With some exceptions, the experience is sterile, brief, cold (speculum included)—and, for many women, shameful. There is little discussion or exchange beyond the very basics of tests and results.

In France, on the other hand, female gynecological health is considered an integral part of the *hygiene de vie*, or healthy living. Women understand that it is essential to see their gynecologist once a year, and most do so religiously. There is very little modesty and shame in a gynecological checkup—both on the part of women and from medical providers themselves.

On the day of my first gynecological visit in Paris I walked in with the usual hesitancy and lack of comfort. The doctor—who was male—conducted the examination with a sense of normalcy and matter-of-factness that snapped me out of my shame mindset and into a state of presence and engagement.

In France, providers expect to have an open and rich conversation with their patients. This also took me by surprise as, immediately, my doctor began a very in-depth discussion with me. When he saw that there was much about which I was not informed, he quickly ran me through the important points and suggested areas where I might investigate further. As a woman in my twenties, he said, I needed to understand certain things that would empower me in my current life and also give me the best chances for health and fertility (if I so desired) later on. He also put the onus on me to be better prepared with questions to shape the discussion next time—after all, my gynecological health was a vital part of my overall health as a woman, and I needed to have a full understanding of what was happening and act accordingly.

For the first time in my life, I felt like a medical provider had treated me as a responsible adult. I felt empowered and secure in what I needed to do. I walked out of his office somehow taller, with my head up, thinking, "Why was I so afraid of that before?"

I left France over ten years ago, and I still miss those visits and conversations with my OB-GYN. Now, in Hong Kong, my experience is similar to what I dealt with back home in Canada. I returned to treating my yearly female health visits as an inconvenience rather than something I looked forward to.

My friend, who is a nurse from France, gave birth in Hong Kong. When the doctor came to examine her one day postpartum, she shared that she was experiencing some pain. "May I see your backside?" he asked.

"Why do you want to see my back?" my friend replied, confused.

With great shame and discomfort, the doctor whispered, "Your anus. I need to see your anus."

"Oh, yes. That makes complete sense as that's where I'm having the discomfort."

Later, she shared, "It was so funny that he was afraid to say it. It is his job, no? Why did he have to whisper to me as if there was something wrong about my anus?"

Pain is not normal

When I moved to Hong Kong, I found a completely different approach to women's health than I had known in France. Some of what I saw was troubling—like the tendency toward extreme modesty in both women and providers—but some of it was highly empowering.

I met Gigi Ngan after the birth of my first child (an experience I'll share more about later in this book). Gigi is a practitioner of Traditional Chinese Medicine and has had some enlightening things to say about what is actually "normal" for women.

I remember telling her during one of our conversations, "Well, you know, there's a certain amount of pain that comes with being a woman. It's just normal."

Gigi's eyebrows rose. "What do you mean, pain is *normal* for women?"

"Oh, not *serious* pain, just menstrual pain. It's normal to have some, isn't it?"

All of a sudden, Gigi was very concerned. "Do *you* have menstrual pain, Anca? Because if so, we need to address it."

"No, no," I reassured her. "I'm fine. But most women I know do have discomfort."

"It's not acceptable to experience any pain around the menstrual cycle. Why would you even think that? The menstrual cycle is like a report card on the health of the woman! When I hear that there is pain, mood disturbances, or other symptoms, I work with the woman to bring her body back into balance. Even the flow, duration, and color must be looked at to understand an imbalance before it snowballs into more serious health concerns. Where there is balance in health, there is no pain."

This conversation blew my mind. Part of me thought she was just wrong—after all, how could the entire Western world, including the incredible OB-GYNs in France, have missed the mark so completely on what is "normal" with regard to a woman's cycle? On the other hand, how could it be that many, if not most, women in the world think it's acceptable to live with pain every month?

Between the sex-related disparities inherent to the medical system and the fact that we have been conditioned to normalize pain as inherent to our womanhood, is it any wonder that some women live with symptoms for years (or decades) before receiving a diagnosis?

The experts agree: women need to speak up

Seeing the incredible differences that exist globally in the approach to and support around women's health made me realize the importance of bringing together a diverse panel of experts from all corners of the world. There is incredible wisdom and knowledge in certain places that women elsewhere can't access.

What I didn't expect was that these experts, regardless of specialty or geographic location, spoke of exactly the same issues around women's health. The consensus among these researchers, physicians, physiotherapists, reproductive endocrinologists, and TCM and Ayurveda practitioners who make up OM's expert panel have different experiences working within cultural norms, but all say with the same conviction:

- Women should not accept pain as a part of the female experience.

- Women's health is not "messy" or to be feared.

- Women's health is not a dysfunction or deviation from medical norms.

- No part of a woman's health journey should be minimized or discounted.

So, if experts from every corner of the globe agree on these fundamental truths, why do women still have such an issue accessing compassionate, informed care?

To me, I think the gaps come from two places: the male-centric foundations of medicine that Dr. McGregor described in Chapter Two, and also cultural differences that put emphasis on certain areas of a woman's health journey but minimize or ignore others.

For example, in France, it's part of the cultural fabric for women to care for their pelvic floor, regardless of whether or not they have children. If you're not from France, you've probably heard of the pelvic floor, and you know it's somewhere down there, but you might be surprised—even impressed—by how much your pelvic floor does for you, especially as a woman. You have it to thank for everything from your ability to stand, to your ability to achieve an orgasm, to the proper support and function of your bowel and uterus. It's also linked to core strength and waist size.

In France, it is so well understood that this organ needs to be maintained in good health that pelvic floor care has been integrated into the national health system. After childbirth, all women receive a minimum of ten sessions with a pelvic floor rehabilitation specialist. This government-funded support is so much part of the process that no one even questions it. These initiatives are led by experts in the network of national healthcare—but it's also normalized by leaders like the current French president, Emmanuel Macron, who recently initiated a strategy to help women with endometriosis get timely diagnoses and specialized care. Women's health is discussed openly in the public space; the result is that women are less intimidated when approaching their providers with these issues.

On the other hand, if you are a woman in the United States, Canada, or Australia, you may not even understand that seeing a pelvic floor specialist is crucial at certain points in your life, because it's not part of how women are educated about health. Regular pelvic floor care is unheard of. One consequence of this is that nearly 25 percent of adult women in the United States suffer from at least one pelvic floor disorder, including urinary incontinence.[2] When I started seeing pelvic floor issues tagged on social media as #momproblems and simply accepted as part of life, I was furious—because with the right intervention at the right time, you don't have to spend the rest of your life peeing your pants. French women certainly don't! Also, mothers aren't the only women with pelvic floor issues. Yes, pregnancy has a huge effect and can weaken the pelvic floor severely, but constipation, asthma, excessive coughing, smoking, and activities like running have also been linked to pelvic floor issues.

If you're a woman outside of Western Europe and you do become aware that you need pelvic floor care, accessing a provider will require effort on your part. Once you find a qualified therapist, you may receive the same level of support you would in France—however, you may also need to pay for it out of pocket, as pelvic floor health is not built into the system as a "must" for female care. It's something you're expected to take care of on your own, and for many it carries a stigma of shame.

In response to this, Kegel exercises have become a bit of a buzzword for pelvic floor issues. They're easy, you can do them at home, and they don't require expert intervention. However, those Kegel apps, inserts, and products that promise to help you strengthen the pelvic floor muscles are actually not widely recommended by pelvic floor therapists, because they aren't actually beneficial for all women! While sometimes the pelvic floor does need "toning," other times the dysfunction comes from it being too tight (in which case, Kegels are the last thing you should be doing). In some cases, the muscle is so weak that it needs electrical stimulation to rehabilitate it before Kegels will have any effect.

Another solution offered to many women with extreme symptoms was a vaginal mesh inserted surgically to correct organ prolapse and urinary incontinence. However, women experienced a range of issues with vaginal mesh implants, including chronic pain, painful intercourse, and *increased* incontinence. The first Australian class action suit against Johnson & Johnson was filed in 2012. Justice Katzmann ruled the company hadn't fully researched these products (which carried significant risks), was motivated by commercial factors, and failed to give doctors or patients adequate safety information. Since then, more than 108,000 lawsuits have alleged that transvaginal mesh causes complications including pain, bleeding, infection, organ perforation, and autoimmune problems.

What frustrates me to no end is that, if women had access to basic information that is taken for granted in France and could ask for the right care at the right time, so much suffering could be avoided.

In this case, the adage is true: how we do one thing is how we do all things. What I've just shared about pelvic floor care could also be said about hormone health, gut health, mental health, aging, and more. Although top healthcare providers from around the world are largely in agreement about the basic care women require to get optimal results, cultural foci and the male-centric medical system have created barriers to knowledge and care.

DR. ALYSON MCGREGOR

Both healthcare providers and women themselves have a disturbing tendency to minimize female health issues. This, to me, is a primary reason (although certainly not the only reason) why clearly beneficial health services, like those Anca described above, are not being accessed and integrated into routine care.

"Oh, it's just menopause. It happens to every woman."

"Oh, it's just my period. I deal with this every month."

"Oh, that pain? It's just my fibromyalgia."

Why, as women, do we feel the need to normalize discomfort? I believe that, in part, this "just-ing" comes from our male-centric health system, which, as we discussed in Chapter Two, has long considered women to be "atypical" men and the conditions with which they contend to be secondary. However, much of this dynamic originates with women themselves, and the layers of expectation and guilt which Dr. Jenkins described. Since most women get periods during their reproductive years, and many experience pain during their menses, pain must therefore be normal and acceptable—even when it impinges on their quality of life and their success at work. Because so many women experience vaginal dryness and painful sex during menopause, these are perceived as things we just have to live with—even when they create challenges in our intimate relationships.

There is no "just" about women's health concerns. Treating them as an afterthought is not only unfair to women who are legitimately suffering, it's also dangerous to their health. The worst outcomes and biggest delays in diagnosis occur around conditions that merit this label of "just."

"Just" means minimizing, and minimal things don't merit

research dollars. Menstruation, perimenopause, menopause, autoimmune conditions, and other conditions that primarily affect women are some of the least researched in the entire medical field. When you read the literature, the conclusion all too often states, "More research is needed to understand these components ..." However, more research is not always forthcoming.

To me, this is yet another reason why women need to communicate their challenges clearly and directly to their providers, regardless of how common or universal they are perceived to be. Even if we don't immediately understand what the symptoms signify, they need to be documented. For example, a CT scan can show appendicitis, but it can't detect endometriosis, nerve impingement, muscle laxity, painful cramps, or any of a whole host of common symptoms. However, because the CT scan looks clear, the doctor might say, "Well, you don't have appendicitis, so must just be your period."

There is no "just" when it comes to women's pain. The more vocal women are about what is happening in their bodies, the more clearly the medical establishment will see the imperative for additional research, updated diagnostic pathways, and greater clarity about women's health experiences.

DR. MARJORIE JENKINS

At the end of the day, we need to view healthcare as a commodity, because it is. Whether you're paying for health insurance (like most in the United States) or paying for universal healthcare with your tax dollars, you are still a "customer" of the healthcare industry, and you deserve to be valued as such.

It constantly surprises me that, as women, we will find a new hairdresser, dry cleaner, or plumber within hours if we aren't getting good results from the one we've hired—but we continue to pay to see healthcare providers who are obviously not hearing us or prioritizing our wellbeing. As I mentioned earlier, we've been conditioned to believe that our providers have all the answers, but if we continue to act as though we have no agency around our own health, we will continue to let others—including the male-centric healthcare system, opportunistic providers, and pharmaceutical interests—drive our health experience. We need to take back control, and that starts with educating ourselves about our health, and about our local and global medical systems.

There are providers out there doing amazing work to support women. We may not always be the loudest voices in the room, but we are there. So, if your experiences and concerns are being minimized or ignored; if you are not getting the support you need to find your version of optimal health; or if you are being prescribed (or sold) products without due consideration for your unique health journey, it's time to find a new healthcare provider whom you trust and can communicate with.

As Anca learned from her French OB-GYN, health is a two-way street. While we work from within the medical system to change the dynamic for women, it's up to women to bring their truth, their attention, and their power as consumers to the discussion.

When women don't challenge the status quo, all women pay the price.

WOMEN WHO LIKE THEIR BODIES DON'T SPEND MONEY TO FIX THEM

"In the nineteenth century, "hysterical" women were sent to an asylum. In the twentieth century, they were put on Valium or Xanax. Today, they're directed to a wellness app."

- RINA RAPHAEL

CHAPTER FOUR

Beauty, Wellness, and The Myth of the Perfect Woman

ANCA GRIFFITHS

The endless and ever-evolving quest to solve the "problem" of the feminine body unfolds, in large part, through the suite of products and services categorized as *wellness*.

For the purposes of our discussion, we will define the wellness market as including diet, fitness, alternative healing, and self-care. Our goal is for you to see how the market is organized and to learn to identity for yourself which products, services, and information will enhance your health and wellbeing, and which may be actively harmful.

As a woman, it's difficult to go even a single day without bumping up against the world of wellness—whether online, in print media, or in person. Headlines like, "Look Better Naked!" "Get Your Bikini Body Back" and "Feel Like You're Twenty Again!" jump out at us everywhere we turn. We are constantly bombarded with messages that tell us what we need to fix, slim, lift, tuck, conceal, and detoxify. In recent years, the messaging has shifted from "be more attractive" to "look healthier and more radiant," but the undertones of "fixing" women's bodies are still very much present. And while the body positive and inclusivity movements have sparked many important conversations, the harmful ideologies behind the majority of wellness marketing remain unchanged, because those ideologies don't actually originate with the wellness industry. Instead, they are a product of the all-powerful beauty and fashion industries.

Why is the beauty industry such a powerful player in wellness?

Since time immemorial, looking good has been equated with health, youth, and strength. One theory is that this is an evolutionary mechanism. We are drawn toward health and strength because healthy, strong people generally create healthy, strong offspring. Whether or not this is biologically true, society has certainly treated it as such. Historically, and across nearly all cultures, men have been able to expand beyond physical strength and good looks by harnessing their intellectual capabilities to get jobs and make money, creating leadership roles, and accumulating land and property. Women, on the other hand, remained subject to the physical definitions of health and strength. Until very recently, women were not allowed to hold jobs, own property, secure credit, or have bank accounts unless their husband was also a signatory. As such, a woman could only hope to look good enough (and perhaps have a large enough dowry) to attract a partner who could take care of her and her children. The better-looking a woman was, the more likely she was to be "chosen" for an advantageous marriage. Her beauty and comportment were the most powerful assets she could leverage to make her way in the world. And, if she was unlucky enough to be born into a family that could not provide for her, her looks could provide a possible way out of a life of hardship and poverty.

As independent, socially liberated women, it's easy to think of this dynamic as a relic of the distant past. But there are still places in the world where women are treated as property, and where beauty isn't just a matter of pride but of survival. Even in more modern cultures, the idea of beauty as currency hasn't gone away, only morphed into a different expression. Good looks and good health are now considered a status symbol even outside the realm of relationships. In today's world, if you can afford to look good, it says something about you. More, studies estimate that good-looking people earn up to 15 percent more on average than their less-attractive peers, and are considered more trustworthy.[1]

It's true that beauty is in the eye of the beholder, but our baseline perceptions are greatly influenced by the culture we live in today, as well as the history of the society we grew up in. Since the beginning of human civilization, certain standards for female beauty have been held up as ideals. While these standards are constantly changing, one thing has remained constant: they are almost always impossible to achieve without harming our bodies and health.

The myth of the perfect woman

In every civilization, and at every point in history, women have been held to impossible, harmful beauty standards. From Chinese foot-binding practices, in which the feet of young girls were broken and bound to change their shape and limit the woman's mobility; to the toxic lead- and arsenic-based whitening cosmetics favored in the Elizabethan era; to that darling Victorian staple, the whalebone corset, women's attempts to adhere to cultural beauty standards have been actively causing harm to their bodies.

Today, our body-altering practices look different—because they've been rebranded as "wellness." However, beneath all the hype, we are still being held to impossible standards that do not promote optimal health—and, in some cases, compromise our health in both the short and long term.

Whoever the "perfect woman" is at the moment, there are products to help other women look like her. As our societal definition of perfection has evolved to embrace fitness and health as markers of beauty and worth, the wellness industry has stepped in to fill the gap of demand.

If you look at the beauty and wellness market through the lens of the "perfect woman" mythology, you will see that we are constantly bombarded with three big lies:

1. Our bodies are "wrong"
2. Our skin color and hair are "wrong"
3. Our age is "wrong"

As women, we've come a long way toward liberation in the last century—but whether we know it or not, we are still making key health decisions based on these negative messages.

You'll notice, of course, that these messages all target things about us that are inherent to our genetics, ancestry, and date of birth—making them virtually impossible to change. Yet, we are told to keep trying. Ironically, when our efforts to change actually harm our bodies (which can and does happen when we try to change what is inherent about ourselves), we do not thrive. This puts us in a consumption loop and actually reduces the chances that we will reach what we are striving for.

Lie #1: Our bodies are "wrong"

It would not be incorrect to say that every major health, beauty, and wellness craze of the last 100 years was created by smart marketers to solve a fake problem.

That problem? That not all women meet current (and ever-changing) standards of "beauty."

Differences in body size, breast size, hair texture, skin tone, etc. are treated as symptoms of a nonexistent but still terrifying disease—a disease of "not-enoughness." This disease, of course, comes with symptoms that only the right products can cure.

Take, for example, the evolution of the "perfect body" over the last thirty years. In the 1990s, the standard was "Heroin Chic" (an extremely thin physique paired with pale, translucent skin, so named because heroin addiction can create these physical traits in women due to appetite suppression and muscle wasting). In an effort to achieve this emaciated look, millions of women young and old resorted to starvation diets. A massive wave of eating disorder diagnoses followed. Then, the ideal transitioned to the "slim-thick" physique (slender, toned arms and legs paired with generous curves) made famous by Jennifer Lopez, Shakira, and the Kardashians. Then, in 2022, an article in the New York Post announced, "Bye-Bye, Booty: Heroin Chic is Back!" Many women clapped back, saying "Women's bodies are not trends"— but, as the *New York Post* rightfully pointed out, this shift is dictated by the powerful fashion industry, and whether women liked it or not, they were about to be bombarded with images of pale waifs across all forms of media once again.

If you think this has nothing to do with you, think again. It all trickles down. From the runways and boardrooms of top luxury brands, to advertising media, to social media, to movies and television, and finally to what is available in stores and online for the average consumer to purchase, messages about "good" and "bad" bodies permeate every facet of our society. No matter how far removed from this we feel, these messages impact our relationships with our bodies every single day.

Then, there are the aspects of our bodies that aren't on public display, but are considered dirty, messy, or shameful. Douches, scented tampons, scented pads and wipes, and even scented toilet papers promise to get rid of or modify vaginal odors, as if they were somehow problematic or dirty. While these products may be popular, research shows that even occasional use can impact the vaginal microbiome, predispose women to multiple types of vaginal infections (such as bacterial vaginosis), increase the incidence of irritation and dryness, and even increase the risk of sexually transmitted infections (STIs).

In Chapter One, we explored the question of why the natural functions and stages of womanhood are only spoken of in the negative. There are many answers to this, but it generally comes down to money. Women rarely hear positive dialogue about their bodies *because women who like their bodies don't spend money to fix them.*

There's nothing inherently wrong with wanting to look and feel beautiful. When a woman pursues the healthiest, most attractive, and most cared-for expression of her own unique body, it can be a huge boost to her confidence, energy, self-esteem, and overall mental health. More, long-term health markers like weight maintenance, cognitive function, inflammation, and bone strength are all positively impacted when a woman takes care of her body.

However, when women's health goals, and their ability to feel good in and about their bodies, become dependent on looking (or feeling, or smelling, or sounding) like someone else's ideal, those goals are no longer supportive to health, and pursuing them may do them more harm than good.

Lie #2: Our skin color and hair is "wrong"

Skin color has long been used as a metric for beauty, class, and social ranking. In many, if not most cultures, the fairer the complexion, the more beautiful the woman is considered to be. This phenomenon is rampant in Asia, where I live. Skin whitening creams containing potentially harmful ingredients such as hydroquinone, steroids, or mercury are heavily promoted and widely used.

A 2021 review published in the *International Journal of Women's Dermatology*, titled "The Dark Side of Skin Lightening," found that up to 75 percent of women in Nigeria, 50 percent of women in the Philippines, 43 percent of women in Saudi Arabia, and 40 percent of women in South Korea routinely use skin whitening products. On the Indian subcontinent, an estimated 50 percent of *all skincare spending* comes from skin whitening products. The United States alone accounts for 27 percent of the global skin lightening market.[2]

This preference for lighter skin tones is a form of discrimination known as colorism. In the West, the conversation around skin color cannot and should not be extricated from its roots in slavery, oppression, and marginalization. Despite major strides in the last few years, beauty standards (and products) remain skewed toward whiteness. In India and Asia, the roots of colorism are often based in caste structures, with fairness being associated with quality, purity, and elite status.

While many major media outlets are making an effort toward inclusivity, and the fashion press has been called out in recent years for photoshopping the skin tones of cover models to match current trends, the "gold standard" for beauty and health in every part of the globe is nearly always pale, even-toned skin.

Hair is another way in which women are made "wrong." From overtly racist standards about which cultural or natural hairstyles are acceptable for women of color in workplaces; to the potent and often dangerous hair products (like relaxers, keratin treatments, high-heat straighteners, etc., which can cause injury to hair, skin, and eyes if used improperly) marketed to help women achieve straight, smooth strands; to ageism associated with gray hair: over and over, we see women being told, "You aren't beautiful enough as you are."

Lie #3: Our age is "wrong"

The large majority of beauty, wellness, and fitness advertising uses models ranging in age from fourteen to thirty years old. Yet, these images are being used to market products to women in their forties, fifties, and above. Rarely do you even see an anti-aging cream advertised with a mature woman's image.

There is almost no time in life when we are expected and encouraged to be proud of our current age. Very young women are encouraged to look more mature. Once a woman leaves her mid-twenties, the pressure to look younger begins. Botox, facial fillers, and prescription serums, once the domain of midlife and older women, are now recommended as "preventive" treatments for women starting in their late twenties.

On the surface, that makes sense: we should start preventive measures before changes occur, right? Only, according to dermatologists, most of the anti-aging products on the market don't actually work. In fact, many topical products *exacerbate* the aging process by stripping the skin of its natural barriers and making it more vulnerable to environmental damage. Long-term use of Botox and fillers may result in weakening of the facial muscles—which in turn causes drooping and sagging. In this way, "prevention" can in fact create a dependency loop and keep women buying more when in fact they should be using less.

According to Euromonitor International, the anti-aging market in the United States alone reached nearly $5 billion in 2021, while the global market reached nearly $37 billion. Despite all the chatter about "celebrating older women," the numbers tell a different story. Regaining one's former youth is, obviously, an impossible goal—and yet, women are expected to try.

This may be best exemplified by a recent issue of French *Elle*, which focused on "aging well" and "feeling good in your body." When I opened the front cover, the first advert I saw was for a pricey anti-aging cream. The model couldn't have been more than twenty-five years old.

The message, of course, was clear. Aging well is great—as long as you look like a twenty-year-old for the rest of your life.

Which came first, the problem or the product?

When I graduated from college, my first job was in the advertising industry—specifically, pharmaceutical and healthcare advertising in the Toronto area.

I was beyond excited about this role. I would be able to put my business degree to good use. I would work in a glossy new office in downtown Toronto, for above-market salary and fantastic benefits. In short, I felt like I was stepping onto a career path I could follow for the rest of my life.

One of the first accounts I was brought in on was to launch a new toothpaste on the market. Toothpaste was positioned to help alleviate tooth sensitivity. It was not the first of its kind on the market, nor was the formula much more different than the existing ones. It was therefore our job to figure out how to make this a necessary purchase for every household.

It was in this setting that I first encountered the tried-and-true formula for pharmaceutical marketing—which, as it happens, is the same as the formula for diet, wellness, fitness, and beauty marketing.

Here's how it works:

1. Identify the product you want to sell.
2. Create a problem that the product will solve. Or,
   if the problem exists already, inflate it to the point
   where solving it becomes "urgent" for as many
   people as possible.
3. Position the product as the best/only solution to the
   problem—first amongst experts, and then amongst
   consumers.

4. Keep broadening the consumer base by identifying new consumer pools with new "problems" for the product to solve.

Now, studies show that, while some tooth erosion is normal with age and wear, it isn't a pressing issue unless a person has an underlying condition (like periodontitis) or really poor oral hygiene. Tooth sensitivity is more often caused by receding gums, inflammation, and other factors that cannot be solved by toothpaste.[3]

The first part of the campaign was to raise awareness of the problem of tooth erosion and tooth sensitivity. The initial ad showed a "test" for erosion where a bright light was shone through the teeth from behind. Of course, there were certain areas of people's teeth where more light could permeate—where the front teeth thinned toward their tips, for example. This is normal; no one's teeth are completely opaque. However, this light test was used in multiple visual ads to "prove" the concept of tooth erosion based on the level of permeability to light. Then, some extreme examples of decayed teeth were trotted out to offer corroboration.

Of course, everyone who was shown this immediate fell into a fearful state. "Are my teeth eroding? What should I do if they are? It is reversible? What can I use to prevent it?" I even found myself asking these questions.

Of course, we had the answers ready to go: the studies (funded by the toothpaste company and conducted by scientists employed by the toothpaste company according to criteria set by the toothpaste company) showing what a huge problem tooth erosion was for average people. Cited were statistics like soda consumption—which, of course, *can* contribute to tooth erosion if a person doesn't follow basic dental hygiene practices, but is not a primary risk factor.

Watching this all unfold was a huge wake-up call for me. I had just witnessed a problem being blown way out of proportion in order to sell a "solution" to the mass market. No one around me seemed to have a problem with this. I felt like I'd stepped into a conspiracy film.

You might be thinking, "So what? It's only toothpaste." And yes, no one was truly put at risk through these marketing tactics. But when that same marketing method is applied to things like children's medication, disease-specific medication, diets, fitness routines, or medical-grade cosmetics?

You can see where this is going.

Needless to say, I didn't last long in that job. In fact, my experience there prompted me to move (okay, flee) to Paris and eventually land my first job in the luxury industry. However, the advertising formulas I learned in those early years hugely impacted my ability to understand the behind-the-scenes of health and wellness advertising.

I recently watched the Hulu docu-drama *Dopesick*, which outlined how the opioid crisis in the United States unfolded as a direct consequence of the exact marketing formula I just shared. This time, the inflated problem was pain, and the "solution" was OxyContin.

The skewed information on pain and pain statistics was pushed to the medical community—particularly in the United States, where pharmaceutical companies are allowed to set prices and create maximum profits on drug sales. OxyContin's addictive properties were grossly minimized.

Now, opioids aren't evil. They can be a huge blessing to people in pain, and they absolutely belong in any physician's pharmaceutical toolkit. The fact that they exist is not the problem. However, the information offered to both doctors and the public on how to prescribe, when to prescribe, and what the side effects could be was skewed to maximize profits, not patient outcomes.

We all know the result: the United States currently has opioid overdose death rates more than twice of any other country. Since women suffer more chronic pain than men, they were, and still are, prescribed opioids at a much higher rate. Between 1999 and 2016, overdose deaths from opioid prescriptions increased by 583 percent for women—a rate 179 percent higher than for men.[4] The economic cost of opioid use disorder and fatal opioid overdose in 2017 was estimated at $150 billion, with an additional non-economic cost of $871 billion resulting from reduced quality of life and reduced life expectancy.[5]

It's clear in hindsight that, when misused, opioids are dangerous. However, when marketers were doing their thing with a new drug called OxyContin, the risks weren't quite so clear. Which begs the question: what if our current "fad" wellness products—like nutritional powders, protein shakes, etc.—are actually the next big scandals? In twenty years, we will have a highly-upgraded understanding of gut health, the microbiome, and the gut-brain connection. What happens when we discover that the "problems" our wellness products were designed to solve were either invented or just plain missed the mark?

This isn't speculation. Just look how thoroughly the science on fat-free, high-carb diets—all the rage in the United States in the 1980s and 1990s—has been debunked. In fact, many experts believe that the fat-free craze contributed to and accelerated the obesity epidemic. What the research said was, "Excess animal fats are not good for the heart, and should be consumed in moderation alongside whole grains, fruits, and vegetables." What marketers ran with was, "Fat is bad." This opened the door to mass consumption of empty carbs, sugar, and processed foods. The result? Massive weight gain and systemic health issues across every strata of society.[6]

Every business begins with identifying a need and creating a product to fill it, and the wellness industry is no exception. Nor is there anything inherently wrong with this. There are many people and companies in the wellness space who truly believe in the products and services they sell, and who have experienced and helped to create real results for real people. Some of these products and services are truly life-changing for certain people under certain conditions; as long as these offerings are actually helping women to feel better physically, mentally, or emotionally, they are filling a vital need. However, even great products can cause harm when used indiscriminately—and, as you're about to see, marketing and nuance often do not coexist in the wellness space.

Marketing the miracle

The formula for marketing wellness products today is similar to (and, in my opinion, largely based on) the pharmaceutical marketing model I shared above, with one key addition: a hefty dose of conspiracy. Statements like, "Western medicine has failed you!" "Doctors get paid to overmedicate you!" or "Get to the root cause of [symptom] that your doctors just don't understand!" are combined with a few big medical terms and impressive-looking citations from select medical studies (which may or may not have anything to do with the product itself), and *voila*! A sure-to-sell marketing message.

That approach in itself is problematic for all sorts of reasons, but it's not the only issue with the way wellness is marketed to consumers.

As you may have observed, the wellness industry leans toward a one-size-fits-all, everyone-needs-this approach. Why? Because the market is constructed around selling you a miracle.

The "miracle," of course, is the *one thing* that will finally help us attain the impossible standard we've been conditioned to seek.

In some cases, the miracle is literally marketed as such: the miracle pill, the miracle diet, the miracle ab machine, the miracle skin cream. In others, the miracle is implied by the headlines: "The One Simple Thing You Need to Do to Beat Belly Fat Today!" or "Get Your Bikini Body in Four Weeks or Less!" And, in still other cases, the miracle lead-in is through the science: "Research Says that Megadoses of [insert supplement here] Can Create a Health Miracle!"

How many fad diets, supplements, or exercise products have been sold as "the one single thing that will change your body and life forever"? I'd put the number in the tens of thousands, at least. Inevitably, this creates a consumer craze ... and, also inevitably, the failure of these products to actually deliver miracles creates a vacuum in the marketplace, into which the next cure-all product can insert itself.

The thing is, each of these "miracles" *will* work for a few people, because that product, diet, or system is what their body needs at that particular time to return to a state of balance, otherwise known as homeostasis. The issue, therefore, isn't that these wellness products are being marketed to the public; a certain percentage of the public will, indeed, benefit from them. Rather, the issue is in the claim that the product will be a miracle for *everyone,* rather than a targeted treatment for a few.

Since wellness companies (like all companies) rely on sales at volume to create sustainable revenue, marketing to a specific niche isn't always feasible. However, when the products fail to produce results for the majority, no one holds the wellness company accountable—not even consumers.

Can you think of any other product or service sector where consumers are okay with a product only producing the desired results 10 percent of the time? A recent Consumer Reports survey showed that, among consumers using fad diet pills, only about 9 percent reported that they lost their ideal amount of weight as a result of using the products.[7] Now, let's apply these metrics to, let's say, a toaster. If your toaster only worked as promised 10 percent of the time, would you consider it a miracle product? Likely, you'd leave a devastating review on Amazon and never buy from that company again.

Of course, our bodies aren't sliced bread, and wellness products aren't electronics (well, most of the time). Everything about our bodies and health is incredibly complex. Nonetheless, the analogy stands: we don't often hold wellness companies accountable when their products fail to produce results. Somehow, despite all the noise around the Next Big Health Discovery, we haven't yet become disillusioned. We are still waiting for the miracle—and still willing to pay to discover it.

This is important to understand in the context of our discussion, because wellness is a huge sector of the women's health market. Research and investment firm McKinsey estimates the global wellness market at $1.5 trillion and growing.[8] Rather than results, this market is founded on the dreams and desires of women (and men, to a lesser degree) to achieve the ever-changing ideals of health and beauty dictated by society and the market itself.

There is no way around it: the ultimate cost of marketing the miracle is women's wellbeing. While, again, some wellness products really do work as advertised, and really do help many people, the overall trend has not been in the direction of enhanced health. In fact, despite all the products, resources, and information available to us, women's health on a global scale is declining.

Life expectancy in the United States has risen steadily since the 1980s for both men and women. However, while the average health of men has continued to improve in proportion to their lifespans, women's health in older age has stopped improving since 2000. Women now account for 57 percent of United States citizens aged over sixty-five, but make up 68 percent of seniors who need daily assistance in their lives.[9][10]

So, what can we do about this?

First, we can stop putting Band Aids on our very real health problems with costly, ineffective wellness solutions. You now know how the wellness market works, so consider turning a curious and critical eye to the health and wellness information and marketing to which you are exposed. Even in the course of writing and researching this chapter, I was subjected to numerous advertisements, including one for a "weight loss patch" that promised to help me drop fourteen pounds in fourteen days. The ad was full of testimonials and expert studies ... and followed the marketing formula I shared above line for line.

So, before you purchase or engage with any wellness product, service, or modality, ask yourself, "Will this actually work with my body, my lifestyle, and my wellness goals?" It's my hope that you will feel more equipped to answer that question truthfully now that you understand how marketing and societal messaging drives our standards and desired outcomes.

The second thing we can do is to be realistic with our expectations. Despite everything I've shared in this chapter, I'm not cynical about the wellness market. In fact, I'm as much of a connoisseur of wellness products as any woman I know. From high-end organic beauty creams to essential oils to the latest nano-supplements, I've tried it all. However, I'm fully aware that most of the wellness products I invest in will not alter my biology, nor will they produce miracle results. They will not give me the perfect body, turn back the clock, or solve all of my health issues. Instead, once I've done the research to ensure that they are backed by credible science and not harmful, I buy them because *using them makes me feel good*—and feeling good is, in and of itself, a desirable result.

IF IT SOUNDS TOO GOOD TO BE TRUE, IT PROBABLY IS

"Our collective experience has shown that when women have the power to make their own choices, good things happen."

- MADELEINE ALBRIGHT

CHAPTER FIVE

One Size Fits All?
Not for Women

ANCA GRIFFITHS

The wellness industry crosses the line from supportive to predatory in two ways: first, in its tendency to market the miracle (as we explored in Chapter Four), and second, in its one-size-fits-all approach to creating and maintaining health. These two energies feed off of and perpetuate one another, creating a vicious cycle of self-doubt and even self-harm for women.

Here's a perfect example of how this works.

A couple of years ago, not long after the birth of our second child, my husband Evan decided to try intermittent fasting (IF) to reduce inflammation in his joints and lose a few extra pounds.

As I'd already heard many people praising the benefits of IF and reading online all the supposed benefits, I opted to do the program with him.

For about a month, we both skipped breakfast, eating only lunch and dinner. Evan thrived on this regimen. He lost weight, and his energy went through the roof. Within just a few weeks, he was adding miles to his running routine, and he'd lost an inch around his waist.

I, on the other hand, was constantly fatigued. My brain felt like it was full of cotton, and I had a terrible time getting motivated in the mornings. More, I actually *gained* a few pounds, despite reducing my overall food intake.

Like most women, I immediately blamed myself. This was working so well for Evan—therefore, I must be doing something wrong. Maybe I needed to work on my macronutrient balance or drink less coffee? Maybe I just needed to push through for another month or two? Maybe I was simply weak-willed? But as the weeks went on, none of my adjustments helped at all.

Finally, I spoke to Tricia Yap, a functional medicine women's health specialist and the founder of Limitless Health in Hong Kong.

"Anca, from what I can see from your intake form, you are one year postpartum, still breastfeeding, and have launched your own business where you work primarily in a different time zone, so your calls are very late at night."

"Yes," I replied.

"Are you also still waking to feed your daughter in the night?"

I told her I was.

"How do you feel when you wake up?"

"Tired. Hungry. Slow."

"So, you're depleted from breastfeeding, your sleep is disrupted, and you aren't giving yourself what you need to fuel up in the morning. This most likely is causing your cortisol levels to be higher in the morning. By skipping breakfast when your body most needs fuel, you are putting your body in shock. This is causing your cortisol to go even higher, your insulin levels to drop too low, and your body to go into flight-or-flight mode. In this state, your blood sugar levels are on a bad trend, and your body will actually hold on to calories more."

Then, she told me something that shocked me. "For most women that I see, skipping the first meal of the day will hurt more than help, particularly when it comes to hormonal balance. Also, fasting sometimes leads women to eat far less than their optimal caloric intake, resulting in low serotonin levels, increased sugar cravings, irritability, and even increased anxiety."

If you've ever felt like reductionist dieting was bad for your mental health ... well, maybe it was.

As it turns out, most of the research about nutrition and diet has been performed by men, on men, and then simply transposed onto women. Recently we have been seeing "metabolic programs" and other attempts to customize diets to women's bodies—but no online quiz can possibly tailor a solution to our unique bodies.

Research on IF demonstrates this gender inequality. Out of seventy-one studies on IF found in Harvard's database, only thirteen include women at all. Beyond that, absolutely none of the controlled studies focused on the female population in general.

When you sift through the precious little data on women in a fasted state, you find something fascinating: women don't respond to fasting like men do. In fact, instead of the much-celebrated metabolic boosts and weight loss, women might experience a 50 percent *increase* in cortisol and a corresponding *decrease* in insulin sensitivity as a result of intermittent fasting. This means that, rather than being a flawless solution to weight gain, intermittent fasting could actually contribute to and exacerbate obesity and diabetes for some women.

We are so used to reading warning labels on pharmaceuticals that we have an innate understanding regarding their safety: if not used properly, this prescription might harm us. However, the wellness industry has no such requirements, and we rarely treat wellness products and programs with such scrutiny. Never for a minute had I thought I might harm my body by practicing intermittent fasting. Nowhere in the literature I had consumed were there guidelines for women, for different body types, or for life stage hormone profiles, let alone on how to proceed safely in cases where there were secondary concerns (in my case, excessive stress and sleep disruption).

Once Tricia explained things, it made perfect sense that IF didn't work for me. There was nothing customized or personalized about the program I used. Like so much else in the wellness world, it was presented to me through internet media as a flawless solution with universal applicability. When it didn't work for me, my first instinct was to blame myself, not question the program.

The fact that this was my default reaction showed me how deeply I had internalized the narrative that *I* was the problem— that if my body didn't behave like other people's, it was my fault. I had been expecting a miracle, and instead, the "miracle" made my problems worse.

Once your eyes are opened to this phenomenon, you'll see it playing out both overtly and covertly across the wellness space. If the latest fad diet doesn't help you lose weight, you're just "not trying hard enough." After all, how could all those testimonial videos be wrong? If the supplements don't cure you, you're not taking enough of them or not doing the "full program"—which can easily cost the equivalent of a car payment per month. If the anti-aging products don't erase your wrinkles, it's obviously because you're either bad at following instructions, or just generally bad at taking care of yourself—not because the product doesn't work as promised.

Again, I'm not saying that wellness products don't work. Many do work, and work well. However, it's impossible for one product to work for everyone who tries it—even if they all have the same symptoms and challenges. There is no such thing as a panacea. Our bodies are too complex and unique for that to be possible.

From a business standpoint, it's difficult to present a tailored approach to a mass market. More, businesses exist to make money. And so, many wellness businesses cross the line from helpful to predatory in pursuit of expanded markets. An oral iodine solution works to help *some* women with Hashimoto's Disease, so why not market it to *all* of them? This fad diet helps to reduce inflammation in *some* women over fifty, so why not market it to *all* of them?

This is why it's vital that we, as consumers, educate ourselves. Sure, wellness products can work—but will they work for *our* bodies at this moment in time?

DR. ALYSON MCGREGOR

My support of products and modalities outside the traditional medical pantheon often surprises my patients and colleagues.

Personally, I use many "alternative" modalities to support my wellness, including herbal and superfood supplements, essential oils, acupuncture, and even energy healing. Depending on the situation, I may suggest that patients research these modalities for themselves and utilize them as complementary therapies to their current medical treatments.

That said, as an emergency medicine physician, I am well aware of the dangers of the unregulated wellness industry.

In many ways, wellness is in a similar stage to where emergency medicine was in the early twentieth century. Research was flourishing, new discoveries were being made ... and savvy drug companies were stepping into the breech. This "Wild West" situation helped create many lifesaving treatments. It also resulted in a lot of trauma and injury to patients who were assured that the new drugs being given to them were safe even though they had not undergone extensive clinical testing.

Today's wellness market has that same sense of excitement and possibility—the quest for the miracle cure-all, the singular element that will erase the chronic issues plaguing women (and men) for good. And, in fact, amazing strides are being made, particularly in the areas of herbs and superfoods. Many traditional plant remedies—from ginseng to ashwagandha to cayenne—are now being extensively studied for use in pharmaceuticals.[1]

However, this "free market" approach to wellness has its downsides. Anyone with enough funding can create a product and initiate research studies to prove the viability of their product, but only a small minority of these studies are actually subjected to a peer review process.

In the same way, anyone with enough advertising dollars and a clear target audience can get their products into millions of hands. I've lost count of how many wellness formulations have been launched by *Shark Tank* alone. Most of the time, the metrics for success are based on how many people have purchased the product—because, "Two million users can't be wrong!" However, very few of these products have been subjected to third-party testing around efficacy and safety.

Unlike in the pharmaceutical industry, the wellness world has no requirements or guidelines around manufacturing standards. Recent independent reviews have shown that the quantity and quality of active ingredients for over-the-counter vitamin and mineral supplements can vary dramatically between brands—and even within different pills sold inside the same bottle![2] Since no one is requiring or checking for uniform concentrations of active ingredients within these products—or that the stated ingredients are present at all—consumers are at risk of (at best) wasting money on a placebo, or (at worst) consuming supplements in unsafe quantities and with added ingredients not disclosed on the labels.

Luckily, we aren't being left completely in the dark. There are numerous third-party certifications that can, if not substantiate a product's claim to efficacy, at least guarantee that it is what it purports to be. The USP (United States Pharmacopeia) is an independent, scientific nonprofit that conducts rigorous testing and offers certification for medicines, supplements, and food products. If a product bears the USP seal, the product contains what's on the label. NSF is another reliable certification; in order to gain the "NSF Certified" designation, products must pass a number of reviews, including toxicology testing.[3] USDA Organic also requires products to pass a rigorous review process, including the tracing of source ingredients.

What's in (or not in) wellness products is only the beginning. We also need to be aware of how, why, and when these products can support us, and when they may do exactly the reverse. The purest herbal or dietary product can still be harmful if taken in the wrong dose or at the wrong time. We also need to know how all of our wellness products interact with pharmaceuticals and other therapies we may be using to heal from or manage disease. As Anca explained above, even in mass-market products, there is no such thing as one size fits all.

It's very common for patients to omit vitamins, herbal supplements, and other wellness products on their medical intake forms. When we ask, "Are you currently taking any medications?" we really *do* want to know everything that you're currently putting into your body. However, many patients don't want to disclose that they're taking the latest vitality formula or "supercharged weight loss" supplement, because they don't want to argue with their providers over the merits of these products. In fact, a recent study found that less than 40 percent of patients disclose their full supplement regimen to their physicians, even if they are experiencing severe adverse reactions.[4]

Many common and seemingly innocuous supplements can have unforeseen side effects. For example, garlic pills are widely used to promote heart health and lower blood pressure. However, garlic is a natural beta blocker and blood thinner. I sometimes wonder how many of the severe bleeding issues I've seen in the emergency department happened because the patient combined garlic supplements with pharmaceutical beta blockers. Another common herb, Saint John's Wort, is lauded for its effects on depression, but it can also drastically reduce the efficacy of many forms of birth control. Taking vitamin B6 can decrease the effects of both phenytoin (a common anti-seizure medication) and levodopa (used to treat Parkinson's disease).[5] Over 60 percent of women in the United States take a calcium supplement regularly—but calcium can inhibit the bioavailability of many types of drugs through a chemical process called chelation.

Finally, many wellness products also do not work as advertised because the research being presented around them is incomplete. For example, Vitamin D3 is often touted as a miracle vitamin for brain health and preventing cognitive decline in older patients. However, recent studies have shown that while supplemental vitamin D3 is indeed helpful in creating a healthy immune response, only vitamin D produced naturally by our bodies in response to sunlight is useful for our brains.

It's vital for women to discuss their wellness regimens with their healthcare providers without guilt or fear of reprimand. If you feel strongly that a natural or alternative product is helping you, I encourage you to share this with your provider. They may not always agree with your choices around supplements and wellness products—and, indeed, may have access to key research and information which may be influencing their viewpoint—but only an open discussion can help you both make informed choices to benefit your overall health. If you feel like you're not able to have a productive conversation about wellness modalities with your current provider, I encourage you to find someone new. There are many of us who are open to and informed about the wellness world, and who will work with you to find the right balance of medical, pharmaceutical, and alternative support.

ANCA GRIFFITHS

Nowhere are promises of a health miracle more prevalent than in the world of diet and nutrition.

Keto. Paleo. Carnivore Diet. Raw food diets, detox diets, juicing, bone broths. Every diet plan out there claims to possess the sole solution to ultimate health and lasting weight loss. And yet, science has proven that very few of these actually support long-term health and weight management. People may initially lose weight while following them, but when they inevitably fall off the wagon, they often gain it all back (and then some).

Why does this happen? There are two main reasons.

First, because reductionist diets of any kind are not helpful except under very specific circumstances for medical reasons (for example, a gluten-free diet for a patient with Celiac disease). When you remove entire food groups for long periods of time (even as part of a protocol like the FODMAP diet), it can negatively affect your gut microbiome and your metabolism. When you try to transition away from the strict diet to a more sustainable way of eating, your body is unable to cope. (Interestingly, professional athletes have some of the worst diversity in their microbiomes because their training routines have them eating the same things over and over again.) Therefore, reductionist diets should only be done for medical conditions under the supervision of a qualified professional, and only for limited periods of time.

Second, when most people "break up" with a strict or reductionist diet, they don't just go back to a healthy eating pattern. They go into full-on rebellion. They think, "I haven't had cheese in a month! I'm going to eat *all the cheese*!" As if cheese is not simply a pleasant thing to eat, but a well-earned reward for months of deprivation. Because their gut is already out of balance due to the diet, the rebound binge is far more challenging for the body to deal with, and often results in rapid weight gain.

Third, stress is stress. If the body is stressed for any reason, it is going to go into survival mode. This means diverting blood from vital organs to extremities, slowing digestion, and holding onto weight. Many reductionist diets cause people extreme amounts of mental and emotional stress due to hunger, limitations, awkwardness in social mealtime situations, and the like. No matter how "pure" the food you are consuming, if you're stressed or struggling, your body reads that as "danger."

Fourth, rapid weight loss is actually very hard on the body. This was briefly discussed in the media after Kim Kardashian lost sixteen pounds in three weeks to fit into a dress once worn by Marilyn Monroe. While it may look glamorous and solve a short-term problem, in the long run such rapid weight loss can seriously damage the microbiome, deprive the body of essential nutrients, and cripple the metabolism (making it harder to lose weight and keep it off in future). Further, many clinical nutritionists say that too-rapid weight loss can trigger non-alcoholic fatty liver disease (NAFLD). This condition used to only be found in people who were significantly obese; now, nutritionists are seeing it crop up in otherwise healthy and fit people who undertake extreme diets and lose too much weight too quickly.

Even diets which originate from the study of healthy population groups are not foolproof. For example, it's been determined that the Mediterranean Diet only works as promised for *people who live in the Mediterranean*. Rather than the food components alone, the diet's success relies on fresh, local ingredients native to the region, and also the lifestyle inherent to that culture. Without the lifestyle components—like leisurely meals with friends, plenty of walking each day, and low overall stress levels—the diet plan is far less likely to create the promised results.

Every nutritionist I talk to, across every part of the globe, says the same thing: "I wish I could just convince my patients that fad diets, diet pills, and starvation cleanses can cause incredible harm, and that they should just start eating real foods!" The truth is, simply eating a diet that includes a wide variety of nutritious, whole foods—organically grown and local if possible—will reduce your chances of developing most chronic diseases by 80 to 90 percent.

Yes, you read that right. Since cardiovascular disease, diabetes, stroke, dementia, and cancer are all influenced and exacerbated by lifestyle choices, eating well can create a huge impact. (More on this in Chapter Nine.)

It seems so obvious when you think about it. However, as D.L. Katz et al pointed out in their 2018 journal article, "Lifestyle as Medicine: The Case for a True Health Initiative":

> "Despite the ample evidence about what behaviors promote health, confusion still prevails among the general population. This is particularly true with regard to diet. Confusing nutrition messages from scientists, the media, the food industry, and other sources have made it all but impossible for any single authority to convey persuasively the fundamentals of healthful eating." [6]

In recent years, lifestyle medicine has gained much broader acceptance among providers—in fact, Dr. Jenkins leads the only medical school in the United States which has integrated lifestyle medicine across all four years of medical school training.[7]

However, we still have a long way to go in terms of public understanding. Since people are conditioned to equate rapid weight loss with health and dietary success, it's often very hard to get through to them with actual solutions. Why take the long, unglamorous route of balanced eating when you can do a celebrity cleanse?

To address this, many nutrition professionals are integrating hypnotherapy and neuro-linguistic programming in their practice —not to coerce their patients into following directions, but to learn to speak in a way that their patients can actually hear. We've all been so conditioned to follow the fads that simple, sensible advice feels wrong, not enough, or out of touch. The overzealous and sensationalist marketing techniques of most diet programs are so powerful that they override people's inner wisdom—and, in some cases, even their common sense. And, since food and gut health are so closely linked to cognitive function and mental health, nutrition experts must consider how to "deprogram" popular narratives on multiple levels, as well as deal with underlying emotional patterns that contribute to disordered eating.

Age, location, food availability, and even income level will of course factor into what a healthy diet can look like for individual women—we absolutely cannot ignore the presence of vast food/ income disparities, particularly in the United States, Canada, UK, and developing countries, where highly-processed foods are often cheaper and more available than fresh whole foods. However, it's my belief that with the right information (and a critical eye toward fad diets and "convenience" foods), most women can design a healthier, more sustainable diet for themselves even with limited food choices and on a limited budget.

One size fits … men?

As I discovered during my brief journey with intermittent fasting, many diets and fitness programs which are marketed to women have been studied primarily in men. In Chapter Two, Dr. McGregor pointed out the impact that this can have when it comes to medicine and the medical system, but this same bias applies to all facets of health, including sports, fitness, and diet.

What does this mean? Simply put, most of the fitness programs out there are not optimized for female bodies. Women differ from men not only in size, but in body composition and hormonal milieu. Our monthly hormonal cycles, with fluctuations in estrogen and progesterone, have varying effects on metabolism, fluid retention, energy levels, and even muscle-building. This can affect our athletic performance in surprising ways.

Unfortunately, when it comes to fitness and athletic performance, women are not included in studies in a way that allows researchers to derive significant or applicable data. In their 2021 article in *Sport Medicine* titled "Recommendations and Nutritional Considerations for Female Athletes: Health and Performance," Bryan Holtzman and Kathryn E. Ackerman wrote:

> "As is the case in many medical fields, sports science research has a paucity of female-specific inquiries, leading to the misapplication of findings from male subjects to female athletes. In 2011–2013, studies published in three of the world's top sports medicine journals (*British Journal of Sports Medicine, Medicine and Science in Sports and Exercise,* and *American Journal of Sports Medicine*) had women representing 39 percent of study participants and only 4 percent of studies were female-only. Follow-on studies in the latter two journals showed continued trends through the first half of 2015; for

example, for studies of athletic performance, 63 percent were conducted in male subjects only, 33 percent in male and females, and a paltry 3 percent were solely focused on female athletes"[8]

Of course, since we are all humans, there will inevitably be some crossover between male and female fitness findings. However, since many trendy fitness programs and products are built on a platform of sports medicine research, it's safe to assume that these offerings are not designed for female bodies, nor built on research which supports female wellbeing as a primary outcome. It's my hope that this will change in the very near future—but for now, women should view them with a healthy dose of skepticism.

In fitness, as in all else, if something is not working for your body, it's highly possible that it *was not designed for your body.*

Take the concept of "10,000 steps a day for ideal health!" This has become the gold standard of fitness goals for many people around the world—but have you ever asked yourself where that number comes from?

Well, fun fact: the 10,000-steps-per-day figure was not based on science, but rather was originally used in a 1964 Japanese ad campaign to sell pedometers. And, as often happens in the wellness space, other marketers picked up what was working and ran with it.

A recent Harvard study looked at 16,741 women ages 62 to 101 (average age 72). Of those, active women who averaged 4,400 daily steps had a 41 percent reduction in mortality compared to their more sedentary peers who averaged 2,700 steps a day. Mortality rates progressively improved before leveling off at approximately 7,500 steps per day.[9]

Yes, that's *25 percent fewer steps* than the common goal of 10,000 steps.

This is significant because 10,000 steps a day is a big number that can be hard to reach, particularly for older or highly busy women. When they don't (or can't) hit five digits, many will ditch their efforts altogether—which, of course, causes greater harm in the long term. According to Harvard research, a mere *fifteen minutes a day* of moderate physical activity can increase your life span by three years.[10] That's a far cry from 10,000 steps, which on average equates to 90 to 120 minutes of walking time.

The key concept in this research, of course, is *per day*. Meaning, every day. That fifteen minutes a day of exercise will not produce benefits unless it's done every day. So while the fancy gym or new HIIT program will say anything to keep you paying those monthly dues, showing up once every couple of weeks and working out to the point of exhaustion is, in the long run, far less beneficial than getting in just 4,400 steps each day.

So, as you are bombarded with marketing about "Boost Your Butt in five Days!" just remember: it matters less *how* you get up and move your body, and more that you find a routine you can stick with consistently.

For me, this has been a long discovery process. I know many people (men and women) who thrive from being super-active (running, HIIT, lifting weights, etc.) but I quite simply don't have it in me to work out at that level every day. So, the best way for me to keep consistency in moving my body is to go with what I really enjoy doing: slow movement and yoga classes indoors, and rigorous hikes outdoors. I also try new things regularly; I'm currently hooked on spinal mobility and breathwork classes.

I used to feel guilty for not doing more rigorous, cardio-based workouts. Now, I realize that these are not necessary for the level of fitness and health I want to achieve. I don't need to look like a fitness model; in fact, if I pushed my body to that extreme, I would likely damage my long-term health. Nor do I need to work out to the verge of collapse to feel like I accomplished my movement goals. I used to constantly reproach myself for not doing more of this or that, and believed that if I only had enough willpower I could push through and eventually get to the point where I enjoyed them. No longer. I have learned enough from expert neurologists, strength trainers, and cardiologists to know that it doesn't matter what I do, as long as I do it regularly.

I'm not saying that you should discount everything you've heard about fitness and diet. However, simply asking questions like, "Was this actually designed for me? Do I enjoy this? Will this be sustainable?" will change your relationship to fad fitness and help guide you toward a fitness or movement practice that actually makes your body feel good.

Influencers, "experts," and social media

The line between trained experts and laypeople who have had transformational personal experiences has become blurred to the point of obscurity in the last two decades. Previous to social media and the rise of internet culture, some level of credentialing was expected from a person putting a new health product into the general marketplace. Of course, there have been plenty of snake oil salespeople over the centuries—but only recently has a person's audience size become a metric for gauging the quality of their information.

Influencer culture, combined with a growing distrust of our

health and government institutions, has given rise to the phenomenon of "experience as expertise." As in, "I discovered this amazing [remedy/diet/fitness regimen], and it worked for me. Therefore, that makes me an expert who can teach you how to get results like mine!"

When put so baldly, it seems absurd. But, unfortunately, "experience as expertise" applies to a vast number of fitness, alternative health, and wellness influencers. These people are passionate about what helped them heal, but generally lack the broader knowledge and expertise—let alone the actual credentials—to suggest or prescribe anything to do with other people's health. Being an expert about your own body is one thing. Being an expert about other peoples' is something entirely different.

Still, their stories are compelling, and people love transformational stories—so, why not try the product?

In most other markets, there are laws and governing bodies that provide oversight with regard to conversation in the space. For example, when Kim Kardashian promoted a crypto asset on her social media platforms, the Security and Exchange Commission fined her $1 million. She was also forced to forfeit the $250,000 payment she received for her endorsement, plus interest. Additionally, she had to agree not to promote any crypto securities for the next three years.

After the debacle, SEC Chair Gary Gensler tweeted that "any celebrity or influencer's incentives aren't necessarily aligned with yours." He said the investing public shouldn't confuse the marketing skills of celebrities "with the very different skills needed to offer appropriate investment advice."

In other words: we should be listening to the people who have access to the latest and best information, and who actually know what they're talking about—aka, credentialed experts.

Unfortunately, there exists no similar regulatory body in the wellness space to support consumers to identify who to listen to when it comes to health, diet, fitness, and beauty products. And so, it's often the case that the person or company with the biggest platform (or the biggest ad budget) also has the loudest voice—and, thanks to the audience size-equals-authority trend, therefore appears to be the most credible.

Again, it's my belief that many, if not most, of the people in the wellness arena have nothing but positive intentions. Many have had incredible personal health journeys on their way to sourcing solutions that worked for them. However, consumers must be aware that influencers and product spokespeople often don't have access to (or don't see a need to access) the detailed and nuanced research available to credentialed experts. Influencers' recommendations may be based on personal results, or endorsement dollars, or both—but they should never be considered a substitute for expert advice.

So, where *should* women go to discover new wellness products, programs, and information?

To the experts, of course. There are many well-regarded experts in the health market who are sharing balanced, thoughtful advice and well-researched products. They may not always have the shiniest Instagram feeds or the most followers, but they are passionate about helping women create optimal health. Such experts are working in every country and sharing in every language. We have begun to gather many of them on our platform at OM.

More, we need to stop being afraid to have rich conversations about our holistic health with our healthcare providers. As I have discovered, and as you will as well, the right health providers will not judge you for trying different modalities to achieve optimal health. To the contrary, they will be open to experimentation, questioning, and integration of multiple resources.

Finally, please remember that, beyond the noise and the hype, good information *is* out there. There are many ways to verify claims made by companies about their products and results. Before you begin any wellness regimen that includes sweeping dietary changes, supplements, or other enhancements, consult an expert you trust to make sure that these will actually support your overall health in the long term. If you don't have a provider you trust, look for information sources and products that are accredited, backed by peer-reviewed science, and (if applicable) certified by the organizations that Dr. McGregor mentioned earlier in this chapter (or your local equivalent). Curate your news feeds and inbox to reduce your conscious and subconscious exposure to hype-based messaging.

And, finally, remember:

If it sounds too good to be true, it probably is.

WOMEN'S CRIES FOR EQUALITY ARE BEING CO-OPTED AS BUSINESS OPPORTUNITIES

"It's long past time since we started focusing on the solutions that actually keep women healthy instead of using basic aspects of women's health as a tool of cultural, moral, and political control."

- MARTHA PLIMPTON

WOMEN'S CRIES FOR EQUALITY ARE BEING CO-OPTED AS BUSINESS OPPORTUNITIES

CHAPTER SIX

"Cash for Care" and the Influence of Wellness Markets on Medicine

DR. MARJORIE JENKINS

I once had a female patient who, when I entered the exam room, announced, "I have no idea what's wrong with me! I have a beard, my sex drive is out of control, and I'm growing a penis!"

After ascertaining that none of these changes were deliberate (they weren't), I settled in to get the whole story.

Turns out, this patient had heard through a friend about the wonders of hormone therapy for menopausal symptoms. Her friend recommended that she see a "hormone doctor." She did, and after sharing her symptoms (reduced sex drive, loss of muscle mass, loss of energy, and brain fog, among others), the doctor suggested that she might benefit from a testosterone supplement.

This hormone supplement was administered four months prior to her visit with me, in the form of subcutaneous pellets (tiny implants placed under the skin) designed to release small amounts of testosterone into the bloodstream over the span of about three to five months.

Well, the testosterone *did* alleviate many of this patient's symptoms, but it also produced a host of unwanted side effects. When I asked about them, she gladly elaborated.

"I'm growing hair everywhere except where I want it. I need to shave my face nearly every day!"

"And what's this about a penis?" I asked.

During the physical exam, I saw that her clitoris was indeed enlarged—a condition called clitoromegaly. From her perspective, I could clearly see why she thought she was growing a penis; her clitoris was so engorged that it protruded from between her labia.

"And then," she went on, "I want sex *all the time*. Like, multiple times a day. My husband can't keep up with me. I'm losing my temper. The other day, he locked himself in the closet. I mean, he loved me being a bit aggressive at first, but now it's putting a huge strain on our marriage."

While we did have a good chuckle together as she recounted how she, driven mad by desire, had wound up chasing her husband from room to room thinking it was all in good fun until her husband took refuge in the closet, there was nothing funny about this woman's situation. She was suffering from a testosterone overdose. Clearly, the treatment she received for her menopausal symptoms did not work as intended, and it was up to me to get this sorted out.

The doctor who had provided the testosterone implants was

a colleague, so (with the patient's permission) I called him to discuss her treatment plan and get more details about the prescription. Our conversation was even more shocking than the one I'd had with the patient.

As it turns out, this provider had also heard about the wonders of testosterone therapy for perimenopausal and menopausal women, and decided to add this as an option in his own practice. After attending a weekend-long hormone education seminar, he attained a "certification" in compounding hormones and the green light to prescribe and administer hormone pellets to his patients.

Now, this doctor was no quack. He was a highly-regarded OB-GYN with a thriving practice. However, he'd fallen victim to the growing phenomenon of "cash for care" services that promise to deliver greater revenues for physicians and clinics by expanding services to key patient groups—in this case, menopausal women. Since testosterone pellets are not approved by the FDA for use in women, insurance will not cover the cost of the pellets, or that of the surgical procedure. All told, the patient paid about $300 for this treatment—all of which went directly to the provider.

As you can guess, a weekend training can in no way equip even the most credentialed and knowledgeable physicians to understand the complexities of working with compounded exogenous hormones—and yet, it was clear that this doctor was confidently prescribing such treatments to his female patients.

I asked, "Can you tell me the dosing for this patient?"

"Oh, yes." He paused to consult his records. "We are anticipating 200 milligrams daily as the pellets dissolve."

I did my best to remain calm and professional. "That dose is similar to what's prescribed for males with low testosterone," I observed.

He was silent for a moment. "It was supposed to be twenty milligrams, wasn't it? I must have written down the wrong dosing recommendation."

I agreed, and let him know that I would explain to our mutual patient that the side effects she reported were in fact due to the testosterone pellets—and that she might need to endure several more weeks or months of these side effects, as it would take that long for the pellets to fully dissolve. Once implanted, testosterone pellets are notoriously hard to remove. Imagine digging for something the size of a grain of rice in the flesh of someone's abdomen or hip!

When I met with the patient, I broke the bad news: she would have to wait it out. In few weeks (hopefully), the last of the pellets would fully dissolve and her testosterone levels would return to her baseline. At that point, some of her symptoms would resolve as well. However, research tells us that physical changes from hormone therapy—such as excessive hair growth and clitoromegaly—are typically irreversible. Given that she had only received one pellet treatment, we would monitor to see if there was some resolution of the physical symptoms.

I couldn't, however, make any guarantees about the lasting impact on her marriage.

Wellness tactics, medical practice

While the patient case I described above is certainly memorable, it's sadly far from unique. In fact, such stories are becoming more and more common in our medical ecosystem.

As doctors and clinicians search for ways to increase their revenue, and drug companies search for new audiences for their products, a new phenomenon has emerged that I have dubbed "cash for care." Nowhere has this trend been more prevalent than in women's health services.

Healthcare systems, and the financial flows within them, are incredibly complex. In the United States, where I'm based, it's an unfortunate truth that many physicians, surgeons, and other pre-scribing providers are paid based on productivity—also referred to as Relative Value Units (RVUs). Therefore, their compensa-tion not only reflects the number of patients they see, but also the level of treatments provided, and the number and types of procedures performed. Not all healthcare providers are driven by dollars, but hospitals and healthcare insurers top the business of healthcare and account for trillions of dollars in annual revenue. In fact, US healthcare spending was $4.3 trillion and 19.7 percent of the national GDP in 2022.[1] The ways in which these entities must operate to collect maximal revenue while reducing costs can and do influence practices and protocol structures.

In the past, this dynamic was regulated to some extent by checks and balances within the system, including insurance guidelines. However, the ongoing lack of research and proper care for women around major health issues and life transitions—in particular, perimenopause and menopause—has created an open space in the medical market, and enterprising providers and pharmaceutical companies have stepped into the breach.

In recent years, numerous "cash for care" enterprises have sprung up in the medical industry to serve patients—primarily women—who are looking for convenient services outside of established pathways. The plastic surgery industry is a good exam-ple: you can now get Botox and Juvéderm from your OB-GYN or even your dentist, administered by nurses and physician's assistants who were licensed—you guessed it—via a weekend seminar. Feeling a little low energy? You can pay for a high-dose vitamin IV at your GP's office, your local hospital, or even a specialized IV "bar" staffed by licensed nurses.

As long as these services are offered safely and with due consideration for the patient's medical history, there's nothing wrong with this. It fills a need in the market. However, this mindset of "cash for care" has made it more acceptable for healthcare providers to offer services outside their core areas of expertise, which can lead to unforeseen health consequences for patients. More, since they are not subject to the same levels of oversight, these types of services are also more likely to be oversold. This creates opportunities for unscrupulous providers to exploit women's suffering during key times of life.

Of particular concern to me is what's happening around menopause treatments and hormone replacement therapy (HRT). For much of my tenure in clinical practice, I focused on serving women in midlife, and specialized in supporting women through menopause. Hormone therapies were an important part of my clinical care regimen—I did, and still do, believe in their efficacy when used with discretion under certain circumstances. However, I also saw firsthand how delicate and variable a woman's hormonal balance can be, and how much care and attention are needed to find the right dose of the right hormones at the right time for each individual.

When any form of HRT is administered by a non-specialist in a "cash for care" or "add-on" environment, the potential for harm exists. And yet, educational trainings focused on hormone therapy for women are cropping up everywhere. Entire companies are now dedicated to teaching physicians how to utilize the slew of

HRT products available to their patients—even if endocrinology is outside of and unrelated to their current discipline. Many of these trainings are trend-driven and based on shaky research. But, because patients—who themselves are informed by influencers, relentless pharmaceutical marketing, and dear Doctor Google— keep asking for these treatments, someone will always step up to provide them.

The result? Husbands locked in closets and clitorises gone wild.

But also, and more worryingly: increased breast cancer risk for women with certain health profiles; mood swings, cognitive symptoms, severe digestive issues, and elevated risk of blood clots and stroke for some women using estrogen-based HRT; new or worsening sleep apnea, breathing difficulties, personality changes, and elevated cholesterol for women using testosterone; and, finally, further frustration and disappointment for the thousands of women who, having been promised a miracle, are yet again left feeling like there is no solution to their current health status. Women who were thriving before their menopause transition get caught in a cycle of fatigue, hot flashes, weight gain, sleep disturbance, and low sex drive—and when conventional medicine fails them, they fall prey to the "cash for care" medical, herbal, and supplement industry.

In short, "cash for care" may fill a market gap, but when these services attempt to address serious health issues for women in isolation outside of mainstream medicine, the results are not always positive. While HRT may benefit some women greatly, offering hormone therapy to wide swaths of the population simply to broaden one's care platform is irresponsible at best and dangerous at worst. Prescribing HRT and monitoring its effects should be a highly-personalized process and should be undertaken only when the benefits to the individual clearly outweigh the risks. Patients look to us to provide them with the best possible treatment options based on scientific evidence. As physicians we take the Hippocratic Oath. It represents a promise that we will *first, do no harm.* When a healthcare provider builds a massive social media presence and leverages that platform to drive women to seek hormone therapy and supplements as a cure-all, the line between "first, do no harm" and monetary profits is blurred, with patients paying a cost they never anticipated.

My suggestion to any woman considering HRT (or any healthcare service) is to seek out a provider who has demonstrated extensive expertise and positive patient outcomes in the area in question. In short, do your research, and make sure the provider has more under their belt than a weekend seminar certificate and/or thousands of social media followers.

ANCA GRIFFITHS

Menopause is a tricky subject. Around the world, it gets a bad rap. And while it can absolutely be a challenging time of transition for women, and can for some women be accompanied by debilitating symptoms, it is not, and has never been, a disease to be "cured."

As we discussed in Chapter One, many natural functions for women are viewed only through a negative lens. Menopause and aging are perhaps the most vilified areas of health for women. Everything about them is viewed from a perspective of loss. "When you hit a certain age, you'll lose your sex drive," we're told. "You'll lose your beauty. You'll lose your mental acuity. You'll lose your value to men and to society." Never do we hear about how menopause is the time of life when women come into their full power—when they step into leadership, wisdom, and greater creativity. Never do we hear about the women who enhance their health after this transition, or have more energy than during their reproductive years, or lose weight once their hormones stop fluctuating so wildly. These things can and do happen, but they're anathema to the way menopause has been branded.

I digress.

Because menopause is widely viewed as a disease, healthcare opportunists have been quick to offer solutions: most recently, the resurgence of hormone replacement therapy, or HRT.

Now, as Dr. Jenkins shared above, HRT can be incredibly helpful for women who are experiencing hot flashes, sleep issues, or other debilitating complications from menopause. However, certain healthcare providers are now promoting HRT as a panacea for all women in menopause, saying that it should be prescribed to up to *80 percent* of menopausal women. The conversation is centered not around a careful and nuanced approach to prescribing these powerful pharmaceuticals, but rather around providers "denying" appropriate care to women due to outdated information around HRT risks and side effects.

In some respects, this stance is a direct outgrowth of the male-centric medical system and its decades (if not centuries) of sidelining women's health experiences. I fully agree that we should be talking about, and finding solutions for, the challenges women face in menopause. However, in this instance, women's cries for equality are being co-opted by those who see menopause as a lucrative business opportunity.

There is certainly money in HRT and menopause treatments. In the UK, general practitioners, OB-GYNs, and other providers are now able to complete a short certification course (the Menopause Care Professional Certificate or MCPC) which allows them to offer menopause-centered services to their patient base, thus increasing their services baseline. In the United States, a similar program is offered through the North American Menopause Society (NAMS), as well as numerous other "training" companies. In many cases, women can request HRT via a telehealth visit, even if they are a new patient to the practice. Some HRT products, like low-dose vaginal estrogen, are now available over the counter in many countries worldwide.

All of this has resulted in a "gold rush" toward HRT. "This isn't your mother's hormone therapy," the influencers say—ostensibly referring to the decline in HRT's popularity in the late 1990s, when two major studies demonstrated a link between certain forms of HRT and increased breast cancer risk. This link remains supported by more recent research,[2] but savvy marketers know that the current generation of peri- and post-menopausal women are unlikely to consider (or even remember) HRT's rocky past, given the recent resurgence in support of it amongst certain prominent physicians.

As Dr. Jenkins shared previously, HRT is a viable and supportive option for many women in menopause; for others, the risks far outweigh the benefits. However, women are being told by medical influencers and prominent HRT proponents that their doctors are *actively and deliberately harming them* by refusing to prescribe HRT at the drop of a hat.

The worst part is not that women fall prey to this messaging —after all, why wouldn't we trust the experts?—but that these proponents of "HRT for all" are using women's very real struggles and symptoms to market a treatment that may not be safe or effective for everyone. HRT is indeed a potential treatment for brain fog, sleep issues, low energy, reduced libido, and mood swings for *some* women, but certainly not for *all* women.

Having witnessed the success of "marketing the miracle" in wellness spaces, medicine is now jumping on the bandwagon—and the media is eating it up. Take, for example, a recent article in the UK's *Daily Express* which explores the claim that HRT drugs can fight dementia. Quoted is a prominent general practitioner with a specialty in menopause and a massive social media following. A scan of her Instagram account reveals that not only does she label menopause a "disease" and attempt to rebrand it as "female hormone deficiency," but also that most of her posts are blanket claims that common menopausal symptoms and numerous other age-related concerns can be miraculously resolved by ... you guessed it, HRT. This physician is, at the time of this writing, reaching millions of women through media interviews and social media platforms. Attempts by the British Menopause Society and many other respected hormone experts to moderate the discussion and draw public attention to the dangers of medical absolutism have been largely ignored by the media, and therefore missed by the masses of women seeking answers. The media, of course, have run with the "miracle" narrative and ignored cries for more nuanced information; "miracle medicines" make for clickable headlines, and more clicks mean more advertising dollars.

Let me be clear: media executives, pharmaceutical companies, and government regulators have no stake in whether you are helped or harmed by HRT, or by any other medical or wellness treatment. Nor, unfortunately, do physician influencers. Unless you visit these influencers directly and obtain a prescription through their practice, they are not in any way responsible for your health outcomes.

Think about that. We now have thousands, even millions of women consuming this marketing and thinking, "This person is a physician. They know what they're talking about. I can trust them"—and then requesting (or, in some cases, demanding) treatments from their healthcare providers without knowing anything about the potential risks, what questions to ask to discern such risks, or if they are even good candidates for these treatments. And, in many cases, if their provider does not fall in line with the influencer, women will go elsewhere until they receive the treatment they believe they need.

I have been unable to find any clear information on how much physician influencers—particularly menopause influencers—are compensated for their promotion of certain drugs. However, there is no doubt that they *are* compensated, and generously. Pharmaceutical companies routinely offer incentives to physicians for prescribing their medications, often under the guise of "education." A 2019 analysis by ProPublica found that, on average, physicians are 58 percent more likely to prescribe medications from companies that offer financial incentives, even if those drugs are more costly to patients.[3]

This overlap between the wellness market, with its rampant sensationalism and influencer culture, and the medical space is worrying, to say the least. However, it is now our reality. Therefore, it's up to us to see through the hype and do our own investigations. To begin, I suggest listening to the specialists in the field—in particular, OB-GYNs, reproductive endocrinologists, clinical nutritionists, and others who have spent decades studying women in menopause.

Of all the red flags we need to watch for, the biggest to me is zealotry. Blind, uncritical devotion to anything—a method, a drug, a diet, or anything else—has no place in medicine or healthcare. When providers lose the ability to see and work with nuance and unpack the available evidence so it is understandable for patients, we lose the ability to create optimal health for all women.

DR. MARJORIE JENKINS

If there's one thing I've learned in my years as a leader in the field of women's health, it's that there is no one-size-fits-all solution for ... well, anything.

Therefore, it's up to women to connect with and work with healthcare providers who do not, and will not, prioritize "cash for care" services over their patients' health needs. When considering a new provider (or evaluating your current one), ask questions like, "Do I feel heard? Do I feel like these drugs/treatments are being offered too quickly, and without due consideration for my circumstances—or do I feel confident that this is the optimal course of action for me?"

It may feel like this is an extra burden being placed on women, but I see it as empowering women to be their own best advocates. Don't be swayed by flash-in-the-pan "experts" or media favoritism. Instead, go a layer deeper. Seek information from sources that honor nuance and women's individuality, and treatment from trusted healthcare providers with whom you can partner to develop a plan designed for your unique healthcare needs.

EVIDENCE IS EVOLVING CONSTANTLY, AND WE NEED TO EVOLVE AS WELL

"Where a wise woman is not valued,
wisdom is lost."

- GIFT GUGU MONA

CHAPTER SEVEN

Ancient Wisdom and the Lost Threads of Healing

ANCA GRIFFITHS

After my first miscarriage, Evan and I decided to try again for a child. We got pregnant again—and I had a second miscarriage.

At that point, I had already started to research how women experience pregnancy and pregnancy loss, and I was frustrated by the lack of information I was finding. Rather than repeat my first experience (and risk getting undermined at work again), I decided to just be open about what was going on. Whenever someone commented on my tired appearance or lack of motivation, I simply replied, "I had a miscarriage last week. I'm not at my best right now."

This approach worked much better for me. I received breathing room and genuine compassion from my colleagues and bosses.

However, what surprised me was the sheer number of women in my company alone who had also experienced pregnancy loss, and who shared their stories with me.

"Remember that time about a year ago when I skipped out on those meetings?" one colleague said to me in the ladies' toilet. "I miscarried that week." I'd had no idea.

The more I thought about it, the more it bothered me that women were expected to simply soldier on after such a physically and mentally traumatic event—and, if my own experience was any indication, to do so without adequate guidance and resources from their doctors, their community, or even the internet. It seemed to me that, if there was ever a time when women should be permitted to heal and mourn, this was it.

I was very blessed that, just one month after that second miscarriage, I got pregnant with my son Rupert. When I discovered I was pregnant for a third time, I was scared and worried. Would this one stay, or would I spend the next twelve or fifteen weeks just waiting for another heartbreak? Was it bad that this pregnancy was so close on the heels of the last? What resulted was a level of paranoia. I didn't know what to eat, so I Googled every ingredient, and ruthlessly cut it from my diet if it seemed like there was any level of risk. I stopped doing sports, even the yoga classes I'd so enjoyed before, because they might lead to overexertion.

I have a vivid memory of sitting with Evan in a café about three months into the pregnancy and having no idea what to order. Not coffee, of course. Toast, maybe—but with what on it? Not cream cheese, but perhaps butter? Still, that wasn't very nutritious, and the baby *must* have nutrients. But if I got a salad, would it be washed properly? Maybe eggs, then ...

My mom pulled me out of this haze during one phone conversation. "Stop Googling everything and just listen to your body! When you crave something, eat it. Your body will tell you. From now on, when you made decisions for you and your child, trust your instincts and stop listening to all the noise around you."

I really needed to hear that. I'd been reading voraciously for months at that point— all the classic books, all the mommy blogs, all the research on fetal development. However, what didn't fully register at the time was that *all of that material was geared toward the fetus.* Very rarely was anything mentioned about what was happening in the mother's body, except where it related to some milestone for the child. There were many mentions of expectant mothers "having cravings," but no suggestions that I trust my body, or that I should listen to those cravings as a source of value information about my own health and nutritional needs.

Yes, it's great to focus on the baby—but during pregnancy and the months after (commonly known as the "fourth trimester"), the health of the baby is intricately linked to both the physical and mental wellbeing of the mother. But nowhere in the literature—and by "literature" I mean Western traditional medical literature, books, and media—does it suggest that we focus on the health of the mother. Take the *New York Times's* Parenting section as an example: the tabs are split into Fertility, Pregnancy, Baby, Toddler, and Big Kid. So are most other information platforms. Where is the mother's health in all of this?

But, again, none of this really registered during my pregnancy with Rupert. Instead (now that I was no longer allowed to obsess over food and ingredients), I switched my attention to birth plans. Delayed cord clamping. Skin-to-skin time. Breastfeeding. But, when it came to how *I* would feel after birthing my son and how my body would heal and what I would need? No one really talked about it, and so I did not even think it was something I needed to consider. I simply assumed I would be fine. The birth would be an extraordinary experience, of course—but then, everything would simply go back to normal.

Once again, my naivete revealed itself in a conversation with my mother, who planned to fly from Canada to Hong Kong to be with me post-delivery.

"Mom, it would be so nice for us to go to the spa for a bit and sit in the whirlpool after your sixteen-hour flight."

My mom's wise response? "We'll see, Anca."

In the weeks before my due date, I decided that I should hire a night nurse. Sure, my mom was coming, but she would only be here for a short time, and Evan's job in banking had him away from home multiple days a week. I didn't want to be alone in our home if anything were to happen, and even in my state of blissful ignorance I knew that being able to sleep would be a good thing.

When I told my Hong Kongese friend Ava this plan, she said, "If you're going to hire a night nurse anyway, why not find a moon woman? She'll take care of the baby, but she'll also take care of you."

I took their advice and met with an amazing moon woman named Esther, an expert in the post-natal healing aspects of Traditional Chinese Medicine. She would live in my home for a full month after I returned from the hospital, during which time she would support my healing and help me care for the baby.

"I have never worked for a Western woman before," she told me through her husband, who was interpreting for us. "The food I will cook for you is a very important part of the healing process.

Are you open to eating what I prepare?"

Seriously? She would cook for me, too? I was thrilled, and told her so.

Rupert's birth was fairly uncomplicated, as births go. Very little went according to my pristine birth plan, and I didn't have the totally natural, unmedicated birth I had planned—but in the end, after twenty-six hours of labor, he was healthy, I didn't sustain any major injuries, and Evan went through the entire collection of Netflix shows he had downloaded.

But oh, my body ...

I felt like I had been hit by a bus. The intensity just would not stop. It was hard to know what to focus on: the lochia bleeding, the vaginal healing, the pain of my milk coming in, my bleeding and cracking nipples, my raging hormones, my disrupted sleep ... it went on and on. Not to mention that I was among the 1 percent of women who develop horrible migraines post-epidural. With all that going on, it was hard to say what was "normal" and what was a potential issue that needed to be raised with a healthcare provider. Plus, with my first scheduled checkup still six weeks down the line, there was nothing that I could do but endure, regardless.

Into the breach stepped Esther.

She spoke very little English and no French, and my Cantonese was similarly nonexistent, so our verbal communication was limited. However, we made do with sign language, a few basic words, and a lot of pictures on our phones. She was often frustrated with me—particularly when I snuck a cup of coffee one morning!—but always in a loving way. She coached me through Rupert's initial feedings, and supported us through the nights when I was too exhausted to move.

But most of all, she cooked for me. And what she cooked was *medicine*.

Despite the language barrier I saw that every symptom mattered to her. From sleep, to water retention, to night sweats, to when and how I was bleeding ... nothing was trivial. She never told me to "just push through it." Instead, it was, "Tell me what's happening so I can understand and help you heal well." I felt that my health was more seen, understood, and cared for than ever before in my life—and I needed it.

Each morning, Esther would ask me about my body. How was my headache? Had I had a bowel movement? How was my mood? Was my milk flowing appropriately? Was I noticing any water retention? (She would ask while looking at my fingers.) Then, she would prepare foods to address any symptoms and support my overall wellbeing. The food was well-cooked (so that I could digest it easily and assimilate the nutrients), bland (so as not to cause irritation), nourishing (because I was feeding both myself and another human), and designed to fuel the healing process that I was going through (high in vitamins and minerals like iron and potassium). It seemed like every meal was targeting a different healing mechanism to support my recovery.

My mother, who had arrived from Canada and was also eating Esther's food, exclaimed, "I've never peed so much in my life!" Esther smiled and shared that, yes, some of the ingredients she used had diuretic effects.

When Esther left after our month was through, I felt like a new version of myself. No longer frail, but strong. No longer weak, but fierce and full of energy—and more at home in my body than ever before in my life. My mind was steady and calm. And, bonus: after a month of eating soups high in collagen, my skin had never looked better!

Of course, I excitedly shared this experience with all of my friends. Those living in Hong Kong immediately understood. Those living outside of Asia thought I was crazy. The more I talked about the benefits of knowing which foods and herbs to take and when, and of Traditional Chinese Medicine's philosophy of "rebuilding" the mother's body after childbirth, the more they just glazed over—or, to my surprise, judged me.

"Must be nice to be able to have someone live at your house for a month," one friend remarked sharply.

"Well, *you* needed that. I was fine on my own," another said.

I understand and acknowledge my privilege in this situation. Access to practitioners like Esther is, in most places, limited to those with abundant resources. My experience simply is not possible for most women in today's world.

But here's the thing: not so very long ago, these practices, and this knowledge, were commonplace in *every household in Asia,* and in the majority of households in cultures around the world. When a child was born, the women in the family knew *exactly* how to care for both the child and its mother; that knowledge was passed down across generations and through family lineages. Only in the last century or so have traditional healing and wellness practices become exclusive and commodified—and their loss is a tragedy for women everywhere.

Where we lost the thread

As time passed, and my naysaying friends and I moved through the journey of early motherhood, I watched our paths diverge in terms of health.

I, and my Hong Kongese friends who had used traditional practices for postpartum support, were generally healthy and strong. In my case, an ounce of prevention was truly worth a pound of cure. However, many of my other friends—mostly in France, Canada, Australia, and the United States—did not heal properly. They never got their energy back. Their hormones didn't stabilize, so they didn't lose their pregnancy weight. Mental health challenges that started in the postpartum stage—like depression and increased anxiety—followed them for years, and some are still struggling. Not to mention the physical complications (like damaged pelvic floors, prolapsed organs, and incontinence) which went unaddressed for months or years because they didn't know that they could ask for help.

How can that be "normal"? Why do women have to get to a breaking point to feel good about taking care of their bodies? And why have the practices that traditionally allowed women to proactively care for themselves been sidelined, dismissed, or relegated to the realm of the financially elite?

I find it interesting that women around the globe are so obsessed with health and wellness that we will torture our bodies with dangerous "cleanses" and reductionist diets, take hundreds of dollars per month in supplements that may or may not create any benefit, and agonize over every last pound ... and yet, most of us don't even consider the simple wisdom of our grandmothers, great-grandmothers, and female ancestors when it comes to maintaining and enhancing our health during crucial life transitions.

True to the miracle marketing formula, lifestyle medicine studies continually "discover" the ancient wisdom of this culture or that one—but often out of context, and usually with the sale of a new product in mind.

"Did you know that eating fermented foods is good for your gut?" (Yes, most cultures have known that for millennia.)

"Did you know that breathwork is good for mental and physical health?" (Thanks, Wim Hof, but it's been practiced in India for five thousand years. It's called *pranayama*.)

Each time research confirms what traditional medicine systems have known forever, the pills and powders and trademarked breathing techniques inevitably follow. However, independent third-party studies on these "miracle" products consistently confirm that the old ways are better because they work with our biology and rely on real foods, not isolates or extractions. For example, most experts agree that eating natural, fermented foods like kimchi and yogurt is more effective than taking probiotic pills. Similarly, limiting your breathwork to a single rigid technique can actually reduce the robust benefits of the practice overall—a practice which was developed over countless generations, and is still evolving today.

***

I was born in Romania during the communist era. My mother and grandmother were steeped in folkloric medicine and were always the first line in our medical treatment. If I had a sore throat, I would get a potato compress. If I had chest pains, I'd get a cabbage leaf and mustard poultice. Teas, rubs, and even spiritual talismans were commonplace in our daily lives. Yes, we had regular appointments with the pediatrician, but going to the clinic for everyday ailments was not the norm.

After we moved to Canada, I became disconnected from some of these practices. However, as a mother, I've come back to them. (For example, chopped onions on the feet are a go-to remedy for respiratory infections in our home.) In addition to helping my kids, these practices connected me back to my own past, and to the traditions of my ancestors. As a result, I have been inspired to explore the traditional health practices of many cultures, including those of my new home, Hong Kong.

In every culture, everywhere in the world, there exists some tradition of healing that can, when applied appropriately and with discretion, support us to create optimal health. In China, there's Traditional Chinese Medicine. In India, Ayurveda. In Western Europe, herbwifery. In Scandinavia and parts of Russia, Sámi medicine. In the Middle East, Traditional Persian Medicine (TPM, also known as Iranian Traditional Medicine or ITM). In Africa, multiple tribal herbalist healing systems. In the Americas, the Mayan and Incan traditions, as well as those of multiple other indigenous nations. In fact, nearly every geographical region on the planet has a rich history of people taking care of their bodies using the natural resources available to them. While a robust study of worldwide traditional medicines has never been done (to my knowledge), I believe we would be shocked to see how much commonality exists amongst them all, and how much the core principles resemble each other despite cultural and geographical distances.

As they evolved and were practiced by laypeople (meaning, everyone except trained physicians), traditional healing practices inevitably became wrapped up in cultural identities and merged with folklore. This created what I will call "householder medicine"—meaning, the stuff our mothers told us to do that, when taken out of context, may make little sense to our modern minds. Yes, some of it may sound silly—but buried within those old ways are sound medical principles and effective cures that could be easily and inexpensively utilized to the benefit of billions of women.

So, how did we get so far from "householder medicine"?

When I consider it, I can find only one answer: the modern global health and wellness market.

As Dr. McGregor explored in Chapter Two, when modern medicine began its long evolution, many of the old ways were discredited as "unenlightened," simple, or even barbaric. In some cases, this was true. However, somewhere along the way, we made the blanket assumption that if *some* traditional practices were ineffective or dangerous, then *all* of them must be dismissed.

More, the cultural component of many traditional medicine systems is actually an obstacle to their use for many people. Here in Hong Kong, the traditional women's wisdom is that a new mother should neither leave her home nor bathe herself for a month after giving birth. This practice is called *zou yuezhi* (literally, "doing the month"). A similar forty-day recovery period is prescribed in the Ayurvedic tradition, which states, "The first forty days will affect the next forty years"—not for the child, but for the health of the mother.

In our busy modern world, a forty-day "lying in" period seems impractical in the extreme. However, that should not mean that we ignore the valuable traditional practices associated with this period—including nurturing foods and self-care techniques like those Esther shared with me, and which served my body so well.

I asked Gigi Ngan, OM's expert in Traditional Chinese Medicine whom I introduced in Chapter Three, her opinion on this wholesale disregard for traditional female health practices. Her response was enlightening.

She explained that these practices don't make sense in our modern world because they were born out of a very different way of life. Up until the middle of the twentieth century, most women in China and the surrounding areas lived without access to electricity, running water, or even basic sanitation. In some areas, toilets and bathing houses were communal. For women in such circumstances, *of course* it was a bad idea to bathe in the weeks after giving birth. That would imply going outside, washing from a bucket, and going back into the house while still dripping wet, even in the middle of winter! More, the water available for washing was not necessarily clean (having most likely been pulled from the local river), so bathing in it could significantly increase their chances of getting sick or contracting an infection. Therefore, the idea of "doing the month" wasn't just a cute idea for women who had lots of time on their hands; it could quite literally mean the difference between life and death for new mothers and their infants.

However, the *medicinal* aspects of traditional postpartum care are separate from these cultural imperatives. We may no longer need to self-isolate to protect our health—but we can and will still benefit from many of the other practices associated with traditional postpartum care. When we dismiss *any* traditional care because the cultural methods of practice seem outdated or unnecessary, we risk losing the medicinal gems buried within.

In other words, we throw the baby out with the bathwater.

Clearly there is a need to highlight and popularize the best practices from traditional medicine systems around the world, devoid of the historical entanglements that might inhibit their practical application. However, there is active resistance to this in both the wellness and medical communities. In wellness circles, it's because there is little room for nuanced application in a "miracle" marketing schema. In our conventional medical systems, it's due to both an intellectual dismissal of "alternative" practices and a refusal to allocate financial resources to study those practices. In both cases, it comes down to money. There's very little profit to be made from traditional remedies because they are so accessible.

More, there's the issue of our deep collective desire for instant gratification, which traditional medicine systems can rarely provide. I'm frustrated by women being taken advantage of because they don't understand how they've been conditioned to look for the Band Aid and leave the big things until it's too late. Why eat bland food and cuddle your infant for forty days postpartum when you can buy a week's worth of detox powders and "get your body back"? Why go out for a walk in nature when you can do the latest fat busting exercise routine that will help you lose ten pounds in five days? Why reduce food intake and focus on natural foods when you can take a diabetes medication to induce weight loss? But what we aren't seeing—or aren't willing to see—is the fact that these quick fixes take a long-term toll on our bodies unless and until we support the body with what it actually needs. Our tendency to minimize (or outright ignore) symptoms until they turn into major obstacles does not serve our lifelong health.

DR. ALYSON MCGREGOR

Growing up, I had an aunt who lived in rural South Dakota. She had a whole farm with horses, other livestock, and a robust garden. Every year, she canned and preserved food for the winter, just as the early European settlers had done before.

One day, she was processing some meat through a grinder when her hand got stuck. She couldn't find the stop button, and the more frantically she tried to dislodge her hand the deeper it was drawn into the machine. By the time she managed to turn the machine off, she had lost all four fingers and part of her thumb.

The nearest hospital was forty-five minutes away. By the time the EMTs got to her, it was too late to save any of her fingers. She was left with only the base of her thumb to help her balance things she could no longer grip.

She healed well, by medical standards. There was no local infection, no sepsis. But for three years following that accident, she was miserable. There were phantom limb pains and nerve pains. She walked with a hunch, her arm hidden by a mitten and curled into her chest so people wouldn't inadvertently bump into it and cause her pain. She was no longer the strong, confident woman she had been before her accident.

When she came to visit my family in Rhode Island, I sent her to my friend Kerri for treatment. "She'll give you a great massage," I told her.

What I didn't share is that Kerri is not merely a physical therapist. She works with muscles and fascia, but also with energy. She can help remove the physical, emotional, and energetic blocks in people's bodies.

I have no idea what my aunt experienced in her session with Kerri; my mom brought her to the appointment, and waited outside while she had her treatment. But, according to my mom, my aunt walked out of the room with no mitten on and said, "Let's go out to eat!" She had avoided going out in public ever since the accident—but that day, she sat at the restaurant and chatted with my mom like nothing had ever been amiss.

After that day, my aunt never wore that mitten again. She stood straighter, and even started using her damaged hand to assist in daily tasks. It was like she had been reintroduced to her hand in its new form, and was able to have a new, healthier relationship with it. Modern medicine had helped her staunch the bleeding and heal her skin and bone, and likely saved her life— but it had taken something more to complete the healing cycle in her mind and heart.

I have spent my life steeped in modern Western medicine. I've worked with tens of thousands of patients in emergency settings. I've written and published nearly 100 peer-reviewed research papers. I believe in our medical knowledge and our ability to help people. But I have never made the mistake of thinking that we know everything.

What I've observed is that, if we (meaning practitioners of modern Western medicine) can see it, we can usually heal it. If it shows up on an X-ray, CT scan, or MRI, we know what to do. If it follows a known "pathway"—such as the well-understood mechanism of a bacterial or viral infection—we are likely to have the most effective cure. Broken bones, malfunctioning hearts, obstructed bowels or airways, torn ligaments, infectious diseases ... if these are your issues, you want to be at the best modern medical facility available. We are amazing at taking things apart and putting them back together.

However, many of the issues women face on a daily basis, including many chronic diseases, are "invisible" to us because the pathways involved are (at least in part) beyond our current understanding. It's a lot harder to diagnose something you can't see or trace. Inflammation, autoimmune disease, hormonal imbalances, and even women's pain are not well-understood by our reductionist systems, and often involve multiple complex pathways that express differently from person to person. In order for them to be healed effectively, a woman's body and mind need to be balanced as a unified system—and because of the rigorous way we approach the science of medicine and healing, we don't yet have the knowledge or tools to be able to guarantee that outcome.

One of the biggest challenges in evidence-based medicine is that, in order to develop predictability and causality, you need to control things down to the smallest factor. Studying complex, chronic disease states with multiple pathways and expressions—like multiple sclerosis, fibromyalgia, or even diabetes—means reducing the whole to the sum of its parts, and the woman to the sum of her organs and systems. Our scientific methods don't allow us to study multiple factors at once. Instead of viewing the whole haystack, we are looking for the needle. This means that we end up with a lot of "inconclusive" evidence and anecdotes, but no standardized cures.

What works vs. what we understand

When Anca asked me how I felt about traditional medicine systems and their ability to help women heal and thrive, I was taken aback. I admit, I'm not well-versed in the diagnostic and treatment techniques of TCM or Ayurveda, let alone Persian or indigenous modalities. However, what I do know is that these systems hold great promise for healing the things that modern Western medicine is struggling to address.

What I think many people forget is that everything in our modern medical toolkit—including pharmaceuticals—has its roots in traditional practices.

Many traditional practices are also being revived because they do the job better than anything else. For example, when you think of "leeching," you probably envision medieval kings being treated bedside by their snake-oil-dispensing physicians. However, in recent years, leeching has undergone a resurgence, and studies have proved its veracity. When I was a resident physician, I completed a plastic surgery rotation. There was a man who had had his fingers cut off, almost like my aunt had. However, first responders were able to get to him quickly, and his fingers had been preserved. After the digits were reattached, our job was to put leeches on the ends of his fingers. (They were medical-grade leeches, grown in a lab, in case you were wondering. I did not need to go leech-hunting in the local swamps.) When the leeches bit the tips of his fingers, they sucked the blood from his hand up through the fingers, thus stimulating blood flow and promoting angiogenesis (the regrowth of blood vessels) in the reattached tissue.[1]

Could we have saved the man's fingers without the leeches? Maybe—but few other blood flow stimulation techniques have proven so effective at preventing venous congestion. Why refuse a treatment that works predictably and well?

In the medical world, we get very excited about new discoveries and evolving care techniques. However, we sometimes forget that everything we know today originated because someone decided to apply scientific rigor to a traditional healing technique or ingredient. We know about penicillin because someone wondered *which* mold on the moldy bread was helping people overcome severe bacterial infections. At the time, microscopes had finally evolved to the point where researchers were able to see and isolate the *penicillium* mold. The mold had always been effective—only now we understood why, and could make improvements to make the naturally-occurring strains more concentrated, effective, and predictable in medical applications.

Aspirin was discovered because researchers investigated the active agents of willow bark, a common ingredient in traditional pain relief. Once they identified salicin, it was a short leap to create the drug we now know as aspirin.

Not all modern drugs are built directly on the backs of their traditional predecessors. We now have enough accumulated research that we don't always need to go back to the source. However, our knowledge of active agents originated—and continues to originate—from ancient remedies. Pharmaceutical companies spend millions, perhaps billions, each year researching ingredients like Amazonian fruits, rare plants, and even snake venom to gain knowledge of their healing properties and synthesize them for use in medicines.

So, when Anca asked me to consider traditional medicine modalities and their application for women's health, my first thought was to wonder why so many in my field have dismissed them. We may not understand *why* and *how* they work—but is that actually a reason to believe that they don't? Or is our current technology simply not capable of tracking that all-important why and how? In twenty or forty or a hundred years, will we finally be able to prove what our ancestors have ostensibly known for thousands of years? It's an interesting line of thought.

The mind-body connection

In my line of work, we see a lot of what has become known as "the placebo effect." It's not well understood, but it has been used to describe everything from spontaneous healing in hospital settings to incremental effects in drug trials. Basically, when we speak about the placebo effect, we are referring to the ways in which the activity of the mind—in particular, a strong belief—can produce measurable effects in the body.

For example, a review study published in the *Journal of the American Medical Association* (JAMA) looked at 3,200 patients with treatment-resistant depression across more than fifty clinical trials. Among those patients, there was a "placebo response rate" of 35 to 40 percent regardless of treatment modality.[2] This means that, no matter what drug was being administered, the fact that people *believed* it might make them feel better was enough to *actually help them feel better.*

Of course, one might expect a greater placebo effect in a mental illness like treatment- resistant depression. After all, it's a disease that largely involves thoughts and feelings. However, what about high cholesterol? In recent studies with popular statin drugs, researchers found that the placebo effect works both ways: study participants taking the placebo (usually a sugar pill) not only experienced many of the benefits of the drug, but also many of its documented side effects.[3] This "nocebo" or "negative placebo" effect is even less understood than its positive counterpart.

While we are making significant breakthroughs every year when it comes to understanding neurological pathways and their relationship to health and healing, we don't have the technology to fully track what goes on in someone's brain when a researcher gives them a pill and says, "This will heal you." We know that anticipation, trust, and belief are incredibly powerful, but we don't have the ability to look at the mechanism of those ... well, we could call them "energies" for lack of a more scientific term.

In short, we don't know why the placebo effect is so prevalent—only that it exists, and that the mind-body connection is a major player in health and healing regardless of modality. In particular, any function or organ regulated by the autonomic nervous system (the same system through which we perceive pain and receive intuitive signals from our body) is particularly susceptible to the placebo effect.[4] This leads me to conclude that our *belief* in a medical system is an important component in the overall efficacy of that system for us.

· So, what does this have to do with traditional medicine systems and "alternative" healing modalities?

More than you'd think.

No probe or scan available to us could have tracked what happened to my aunt on Kerri's physical therapy table that day—and yet, she walked out of that office a healed woman. Similarly, none of our observational techniques have been successfully applied to traditional medicine practices like TCM or Ayurveda. These practices tend to be highly customized, taking into account the holistic picture of an individual's health state, constitution, and even personality; this makes them hard to study except on a single-case basis, which carries far less weight in a system where double-blind, randomized, highly-controlled studies are the norm.

Because they are so difficult to study, Western medicine has dismissed traditional medicine systems as being unscientific or haphazard. However, it's possible that the opposite may be true, because when studies are crafted to analyze *results* rather than dissect pathways, we see that traditional medicine practices consistently produce positive results for patients, particularly those with chronic or hard-to-treat conditions like autoimmune disease, diabetes, chronic pain, anxiety, or depression. In China, Traditional Chinese Medicine is applied in both preventative capacities and for the treatment of such chronic conditions, with great success;[5] we are now starting to see such integrations in hospitals elsewhere in the world.

Nevertheless, in my research for this chapter, I noticed an interesting phenomenon: while traditional modalities did indeed produce positive results for patients with hard-to-treat conditions, the results were often *even better* when traditional modalities were applied in combination with modern Western treatments.

How to use traditional medicine to support your health

Before we get into specifics, I want to direct your attention back to the placebo effect. If you believe it will help you, it's likely that it can—at least on some level. If pursuing a traditional medicine healing pathway in conjunction with your modern medical treatment plan feels good to you, you should absolutely explore it. We own our bodies. We should feel empowered to do our own research, ask questions, and take steps to heal ourselves, whatever that looks like to us.

I suggest that you consider what I've shared in this chapter when making your decisions regarding your treatment pathways. For emergencies and acute concerns, modern Western medicine is absolutely the way to go. Acupuncture and herbs are not going to save you if you're having a heart attack, just got in a car accident, or had your fingers shredded in a meat grinder. However, if you have chronic conditions, are not getting a conclusive diagnosis through modern Western medical pathways, or your conditions are not responding to conventional treatments, alternative therapies (including traditional medicine systems) might be a good choice for you.

Regardless of how you choose to engage with conventional and alternative therapies, and which therapies you choose, I encourage an open dialogue with all of your providers. If you are taking statin drugs, blood thinners, or pain medication, for example, your traditional health provider absolutely needs to know so they can tailor herbal prescriptions and other treatments accordingly. If your Traditional Chinese Medicine provider has recommended a suite of herbs to help manage your blood sugar, your GP and specialists should be informed so they don't prescribe something that could cause an interaction. Even if you're utilizing bodywork and massage, you should be transparent about your other health pathways so your therapist can consider how best to work with you.

In my personal experience, I've found that most patients will disclose their conventional prescriptions to their alternative practitioners but won't disclose their herbal prescriptions to their physicians. As we've explored in previous chapters, an open dialogue is the best way to advocate for yourself and your health. Also, it's okay to educate your physician about traditional medicine—especially if you're seeing measurable results. Doctors are taught to be investigative, but we can only help to the degree that you are willing to share what's going on. Who knows: your conversation might even inspire your doctors to further collaboration between disciplines.

If you can't share your traditional or alternative health practices with your providers, this indicates a lack of trust. In such a case, it's best to look for a provider you can have an open conversation with. If you're in an area without a lot of options, you could explore telemedicine or virtual medicine to connect with someone who will respect your choices and work with you to find the best pathways for your health.

A final aside …

I actually dislike the word "tradition." There are lots of "traditional" things within cultures, and even in medicine, that should be ousted. For instance, consider genital mutilation, the systemic minimization of women and women's experiences (including in healthcare), and strident religious beliefs which prevent people from seeking adequate care during health emergencies.

So, while we designate many ancient modalities as "traditional"—Traditional Chinese Medicine, Traditional Persian Medicine, etc.—I would actually encourage people to stop thinking of them as "traditions." From my understanding, these are not unchanging, antiquated institutions, but rather living bodies of knowledge that have been practiced and improved on for hundreds of generations. As modern providers trained in rigorous scientific methods, we can examine and test this information over time and, as our understanding and technology grows, come to appreciate ever more deeply what this accumulation of human wisdom has to offer.

Evidence is evolving constantly—and we must evolve as well.

ANCA GRIFFITHS

Despite the fact that traditional "householder medicine" practices have been largely lost, most people have heard of at least one traditional medicine system. In the United States, basic Ayurvedic practices have been embraced by the yoga and wellness communities, and certain aspects of TCM are utilized as supplementary and preventative care pathways by hospitals and cancer clinics in China and elsewhere.

However, the public knowledge base when it comes to these traditions is, to put it generously, diluted.

Many simple practices—for example, skin care practices like Gua Sha (skin scraping) or *abhyanga* (the Ayurvedic practice of self-massage with oil)—have been co-opted and commodified by influencers and wellness companies. However, the rich knowledge behind these practices never makes it into the Instagram ads. The same applies to the nutrition and diet space: a basic understanding of "warming" and "cooling" foods does not an Ayurvedic expert make.

Traditional medicine systems, regardless of where they originate, are nuanced and deep, and while there are many people out there who practice them to varying degrees, true experts are often harder to find.

There are numerous barriers that prevent average women from connecting with true traditional healing practices. In the United States in particular, regulations often restrict how and where traditional healers can practice their art—including how bodywork can be practiced, what herbs can be prescribed, and what advice can be given. In other parts of the world, availability, language barriers, and widespread quackery have made it harder for women to access quality services.

If you are interested in learning more about how to properly care for your body through a system of traditional medicine, my advice is to circumvent the online noise and go right to an accredited expert—preferably someone who has studied their healing modality in depth in its country of origin (or at least, whose primary teachers and certifiers are from that country). In China, at least six years of intensive study are required to practice TCM. In India, the traditional Ayurvedic schools may require up to eight years and thousands of hours of training. What these experts can provide is far different than what is offered by the average online health coach—in part because they have enough clinical experience to know the difference between what practices have a true medical origin (versus a cultural origin). Essentially, it's the difference between a doctor who specializes in endocrinology versus an internet influencer who hopped on the hormone train.

VITALITY AND PEACE
CAN NEVER COME
FROM A BOTTLE

"The history of all times, and of today
especially, teaches that ... women
will be forgotten if they forget
to think about themselves."
- LOUISE OTTO-PETERS

CHAPTER EIGHT

Diagnosing Our Beliefs

DR. MARJORIE JENKINS

On the morning I intended to write my portion of this chapter, I had a powerful realization.

As a strong, independent, highly-successful woman, I don't tend to ask for help.

Perhaps it is because our society, while progressing past binary gender, still pushes gender norms onto boys and girls early. Boys have blue dump trucks and red race cars. Girls have Barbies, baby dolls, and toy kitchens. At an early age, girls are conditioned to be taking care of something, to be nurturing. Even without knowing it, many of us hold onto that into adulthood. Suddenly, the baby doll and easy bake is replaced by all the various things on our plates as working women, mothers, spouses, and caretakers.

I have three children, two of whom are women. I have always hoped that they would grow into strong, smart, independent, and capable individuals—and they have! I never wanted them to be stuck in a relationship that didn't work for them because they needed to be supported, financially or otherwise. Rather than teaching them to rely on others, I taught them to figure things out for themselves and I led by example. In many ways, this was absolutely the right thing to do. My daughters have far more choices than most of the women I grew up with in Appalachia.

I know I'm not the only parent who raised their daughters in this way. It was a natural evolution from an independent career woman who became a mom. Why, then, am I surprised when women like us don't suddenly evolve in adulthood to people who proactively ask for assistance in life—be it health or otherwise?

In my years as a clinician, I helped many patients who came to me exhausted and defeated. When we looked beyond the symptoms to what was going on in their lives, we found that they were carrying a disproportionate load in their households, in their relationships, and at work. I could assist them to alleviate some of their symptoms, but no pill or injection could give them more time in their day.

We women are too often like the kittens on those motivational posters, clinging to a rope with one paw while the caption shouts in bold lettering, "Don't give up! You've got this!" The women in my clinic were clinging to their independence and "superwoman" image for dear life, and it was not in their nature to ask anyone outside of the exam room to extend a hand their way.

One of the biggest reasons women are failing at health is

that they have never learned how to ask for what they need, or how to say no. From the time we are given those baby dolls and told, "Don't forget to give her the bottle, sweetie!" we are taught that thinking of others before ourselves makes us "good" people. So, when we are asked to serve on this committee, manage that fundraiser, take on this extra project at work, we say, "I can do that." Before we know it, we're managing twenty-hour days, and walking around like shells of ourselves.

This is where my mind was this morning.

I looked at myself in the mirror and realized that, after navigating (and beating) breast cancer and the associated treatments in 2022 and early 2023, my body is exhausted and traumatized. Those who encounter trauma early in life learn to compartmentalize events and memories. We tuck them away and do not dwell on them. This isn't conscious, it's a reflexive survival tendency. It was clear to me on this Monday morning that I had yet to slow down enough to work through how the past year had impacted me, physically, mentally, and emotionally.

And, as of this morning, not a soul knows the above.

I am a leader whom many would view as having broken through the glass ceiling. I have worked diligently to achieve and create the footprint I wish to leave behind in my life and career. I have been involved in clinical care, health policy, biomedical research, and education. I am a mother, a wife, a sister, a daughter, a friend, and a community leader. I have resources and support networks and plenty of people who care about me. And yet, I didn't drive to work this morning thinking, "Who can I talk to about this morning's revelation?" Instead, I decided to do what many of us do in these instances, and told myself, "I will address it when I have time, but for now I need to go about business as usual."

Yet, now that the thought has made itself known, it won't go away.

The thing that makes this all so hard is that, from all outward appearances, I am the same as my pre-cancer self. I kept most of my hair. My energy is improving every day. I don't have outward signs of scarring or disfigurement. To most of those I engage with daily, I'm back to being who I was before, or never really changed in the first place.

I wonder: do we think it is feasible to go through a challenging journey, whether related to health or some other life-changing event, without coming out on the other side as "different"? I have counseled and cared for many women who seem to have done so. I do have physical scars that are visible to me, reminding me daily of how truly blessed I am to be alive and healthy, and serving as a daily reminder of how different my 2023 self is.

There is something to the saying "physician, heal thyself"— which means, in essence, before we correct others, make sure we aren't making the same or similar choices. The majority of students in higher education and medical school today are women. As leaders in the space, I and my colleagues remind our students that there are resources available to them if they need them. In presenting myself as strong and resilient, what I'm *not* doing is showing them through action that it's okay to seek out resources, or to take the time to recover after a stressful life event. Instead, I have, perhaps subconsciously, done my best to minimize my journey so that no one has any reason to view me as less than complete, or to question my ability to lead.

If I, a lifelong proponent for women's health with a nuanced clinical knowledge base, find myself in this new awareness, yet choose not to utilize the support system and resources available, how can I expect other women to do any differently?

As women, we are our own harshest critics, and seem to always find ourselves wanting in some respect. I spent time this morning dissecting my epiphany, but had to admit that I would be letting down so many people, both seen and unseen, if I were to slow down on the busy highway that is my life.

On the other hand, I do know that if I don't address this issue, it may have a detrimental impact on my health. If I didn't have the clinical knowledge and the training to recognize the layers of mental and physical symptoms I'm experiencing, I would have probably woken up this morning thinking, "I'm exhausted. Maybe I need vitamins." It's possible that I then would have pulled out my credit card and dropped an obscene amount of money on the latest and greatest supplements to help me "get my energy back." Maybe I would have made an appointment with my general practitioner, who would look for the concrete manifestations of disease, and who would likely find nothing. And through it all, I would keep hoping that, one day in the future, if I could just find the right solution, I would wake up feeling like myself again. Yet, without changing something fundamental about the way I've been living my life—without addressing the beliefs that lie beneath all the levels of my experience—that would probably never happen. Despite all our amazing technologies and advancements, the level of vitality and peace that I and millions of other women are looking for can never come from a bottle.

Who do we believe we are?

In order to create optimal health as women, we need to understand not only how the market works, but how *we* work.

In this book, we have touched on the conditioning that we as women receive around beauty, fitness, and aging, and how these can set us up to receive incomplete care and fall prey to predatory practices in both the wellness and medical industries. However, there is another layer of conditioning that we need to examine if we want to truly create a pathway to wellbeing, and that is our internalized belief systems about who women are, and what women can and cannot—and should and should not—do.

For some women, this shows up as I've described above: through a driving need to be all things to all people, or to push through illness without appearing weak. For women with chronic conditions that impact their daily functioning, it might feel like shame at their inability to caretake others or contribute as expected. Again, it goes back to this idea that women need to be everything to everyone, all the time—to be "perfect" in both appearance and action.

The first step to overcoming the internalized beliefs that impact our health is to realize that they are there. No matter how much of a rebel you are, chances are you've received and are still dealing with some level of societal or familial conditioning around what it means to be a woman. Recognize if you have been conditioned to hide, minimize, or explain away aspects of your health journey to avoid being alienated or seen as weak. Recognize where you may be equating not being heard by your providers with being overdramatic or mistaken about what is happening in your body. Recognize where you may be falling for "miracle marketing" tactics or searching for a panacea to solve your health problems so you can continue to pursue an unattainable ideal of perfection or productivity. Such realizations are rarely easy and often painful, but they are necessary if you are to create true health and wellbeing for your unique body in your current stage of life.

The second step is realizing which of your beliefs are actually valid and demand a new solution or course of action. Many women who are afraid of facing doubt or ridicule at the hands of their providers aren't operating from assumptions, but from experience. The solution to this is, of course, to find new providers, not hide or minimize symptoms—but first, it's to eradicate the ingrained belief that the provider is somehow superior in the equation. Doctors and healthcare providers are highly-educated individuals with a huge knowledge base, but they're also human beings who carry their own experiences, biases, and insecurities. When you enter into a relationship with a provider, they become a *partner* in your health, not some stethoscope-wielding overlord.

The "forever" complex

The final, and perhaps most limiting, belief that women carry about their health is this: "I will feel this way forever, so I must learn to live with it."

This belief, which I've dubbed the "forever complex," actually stems from our subconscious need to establish permanence and is closely related to our innate resistance to change. When we believe we know what will happen, we can plan around it, adapt to it. We become committed to "living with" whatever is occurring because to do otherwise feels unsafe.

Of course, all of this is happening subconsciously. On a conscious level, we tend to believe that there is always something better on the way—or, at least, that something better exists. We might even make some surface-level or short-term changes. We hope that things will get better for us. We hope that we will come through unscathed. We hope that we will find a solution to our health challenges, finally lose the weight, finally be able to feel like ourselves again.

Yet, that deeper part of us whispers, "But what if you *don't*?"

Psychologists describe this phenomenon as *competing commitments*. In medicine, we see this all the time. There are the overt cases, of course: the patient with COPD who continues to smoke, the heart patient who refuses to scale back on their high-stress lifestyle, the ultra-athlete who can't stay on the couch long enough for her ACL to heal properly. These people all vocalize their commitment to healing, but their *other* commitments—in the above cases, to maintaining a comforting habit, meeting the demands of a high-powered job, or maintaining an image of competitive strength—get in the way of their commitment to heal.

Then, there are the more subtle cases of competing commitments, which often manifest as opposition. In clinical practice, I had many patients who might have benefited greatly from a short-term course of antidepressants or anti-anxiety medications but refused to take that treatment path. "Once you're on those, you're on them forever," one woman said to me. As if, by making the choice that would support them in the present moment, they would somehow be creating a fixed, irreversible state of being that would alter their entire lives.

Often, the "forever complex" kicks in after a diagnosis. Women think, "I have this disease/syndrome/condition now, and so I will have to live with it always." The narrative in medicine furthers this; for example, when a new drug is prescribed, there is often no discussion about what it would take to reduce the need for the drug, or eliminate it altogether. This can sabotage the care process by creating competing commitments around lifestyle changes and treatment pathways—after all, if you're *always* going to have Type 2 diabetes, and you're *always* going to need to take metformin, why bother cutting out sugar and carbs? If you're *always* going to pee your pants after childbirth, why bother with the pelvic floor specialist?

When looked at boldly, this "forevering" is illogical, even nonsensical. Yet, it's one of the most common challenges for women who want to get, and stay, well. When your instinct to adapt to this new reality kicks in, it creates a dissonance in your inner narrative. You become simultaneously committed to living with your condition as it is currently expressed, and to overcoming and getting back to the way things were before. In such a state, how can any positive progress be made?

I often tell patients, "If you don't find a way to control this disease, it will control you." We could easily alter that to say, "If you don't control your health, it will control you." Controlling something is different than simply accepting it—but to control your health, you first must recognize where you might have competing commitments and do what it takes to shift your priorities. If you want to move the needle with regard to your health, you can't be simultaneously committed to wishful thinking and proactive action. You can't be simultaneously committed to being invincible and receiving help to heal. You can't be simultaneously committed to being sick and being well.

In order to identify competing commitments and change the beliefs that are keeping us from healing, we need support. Modalities like Cognitive Behavioral Therapy (CBT) can be helpful in changing belief patterns and habitual behaviors. It often takes another person's perspective to show us where our beliefs and behaviors don't line up with our desired outcomes. Once we see it clearly, it's easier to take steps in the right direction.

ANCA GRIFFITHS

Life is full of challenges, and many—if not most—of them affect our health in some way. On the outside, we may appear healthy, vibrant, and put together. But on the inside, we may be struggling, stressed, or even dealing with a major health crisis.

To me, this is indicative of two things.

One, we need to be more transparent so that we can ask for and receive help when we need it. As Dr. Jenkins shared above, this can be a huge challenge for women in positions of leadership and influence—but if we don't start stepping into the discomfort of being open about our struggles, nothing ever changes, and we are left to bear the burden alone. As Michelle Obama said in a 2018 interview on *Good Morning America*: "I think it's the worst thing that we do to each other as women, not share the truth about our bodies and how they work, and how they don't work ... We sit in our own pain thinking that somehow we are broken." Obama was referring to her miscarriage, and after my own pregnancy losses I understand her words deeply. However, her wise words can be applied to all women's health struggles. When we keep it to ourselves, we suffer alone.

Two, we need to be kinder to ourselves and to other women. We are always our own harshest critics. Our brains are wired to look for flaws and dangers so we can repair them; this tendency is part of our survival mechanism. However, we can consciously choose to override this and cultivate greater compassion and generosity toward ourselves and others as part of our overall health journey.

When I began to consider this concept of kindness, the first person who came to mind was my mother.

As I shared earlier in this book, I grew up in Communist Romania. My mother raised me in one of the harshest political and social climates in 1980s Europe. Every day, our safety was at risk, and we had to fight for everything we had. Being a young child, I had very little perspective around what my mother had to go through every day just to keep me fed, clothed, and safe.

When we emigrated to Canada after the revolution, my mother was forty years old and spoke no English. We lived in the Toronto area for nearly six years as illegal immigrants, which presented a whole new set of stressors. She had to rebuild her life with little to no structural support, and with me relying on her.

And yet, when she looks back at that period, she doesn't celebrate how strong, dedicated, and brave she was. She doesn't acknowledge how much strain her body and mind had to endure without respite for decades and decades. Instead, she sees her many health challenges—like anxiety, panic attacks, and her challenging transition through menopause—as her fault, often saying that perhaps she could have done things differently to have better outcomes. She wonders, watching me with my own children, how she could have done things differently with me.

"Mom," I remind her, "you did everything for me. You kept me alive! You moved halfway across the world to give us a future. How could you have done 'better' than that?"

In her, I see the tendency of women to carry the weight of the world. In many cultures and places, women are responsible for it all: family, religion, food, the home, and everyone else's mental health. This belief that, "It's a woman's job to carry on," once permeated everything, and is still with us in many ways. Think about it: when something goes wrong with the child or the family, who gets blamed? The mother. When a man is unhappy in his marriage, who gets blamed? The wife. When a woman's health is less than optimal, who gets blamed? She does. And, for all the detriments of a patriarchal society, women can be just as hard on themselves and one another as the institutions are on them collectively.

Just look at the comments on any health expert's social media accounts. You'll see women insulting the expert for not being thinner and prettier, or for falling short in some superficial way. You'll see women insulting each other for their unique health choices, making blanket statements about other women's experiences, and generally being cruel.

To what end? And when does it stop?

That's why, to me, the best approach is always kindness—to ourselves, and to one another. Nothing gets better when we are unkind. No problem is solved by pointing out why a woman is "bad," ignorant, or unworthy. No health or wellbeing is reclaimed through cruelty.

To me, the belief that presents the biggest obstacle to women winning at health is the belief that we cannot love and be kind to ourselves—the belief that we are always, somehow, falling short and need to be punished for it. When we allow ourselves to step back and realize how incredible we truly are, we make space for more kindness and compassion to come through. And, when we learn to be kind to ourselves, it becomes easier to be kind to others.

When judgment and self-hatred disappear, we make space to feel gratitude to our bodies for taking us through those tough moments—through the intense work or family situations, the health challenges, the grief and loss, and the joy as well. And *that* is healing.

NOW THAT YOU KNOW, WHAT WILL YOU DO?

"The challenge is not to be perfect,
it's to be whole."

- JANE FONDA

CHAPTER NINE

But, We Can

ANCA GRIFFITHS

I can't tell you how many times women from around the world have approached me after a presentation or live masterclass and said, "If only I'd known about this when ..."

Until this point, my goal—and the goal of my coauthors—has been to bring your attention to the factors that stand between you and your optimal health. As you now understand, male-centric medicine, the predatory wellness industry, and the commodification and marginalization of traditional practices have made it challenging for women to win at health on both personal and collective levels. And, as with the flow of our discussion on these pages, we've seen how everything about our experience of the global healthcare market starts and ends with our beliefs.

When it comes to our wellbeing, we live at and operate from a crossroads: the place where the global health marketplace, our individual health, and our understanding of what it means to be a woman meet and overlap. Hopefully, this book has opened your eyes to the various dynamics that might be influencing and impacting the above factors, and given you a deeper, more nuanced understanding of why women aren't winning at health on a global level.

Our goal in this book has been to empower you with knowledge, perspective, and perhaps a bit of righteous anger. But now that you know, what can you *do* about it?

The title of this book is *Why Women Aren't Winning at Health (but can)*.

So, let's talk about the "but can."

The six pillars of optimal health for women

As of this writing, I've created and facilitated over 150 masterclasses with over 100 experts in all areas of health—from modern Western medicine (including physicians, specialists, physiotherapists, osteopaths, and educators) to Traditional Chinese Medicine and Ayurveda practitioners, breathwork experts, nutritionists, fitness experts, and more. These masterclasses cover a wide variety of subjects including: diet and nutrition, mental health, breathwork, heart health, and many other modalities.

All of our experts have two things in common. First, they are highly accredited in their fields, have extensive clinical experience, and have created real results for real patients. Second, they do not sell products, pharmaceuticals, or "cash for care" services as a primary means of income; they understand and utilize the tools that are out there, but they are not financially motivated to recommend them to patients or students.

When you bring experts like these together to talk about what optimal health for women looks like ... well, let's just say I was shocked.

When I first began this project, I expected experts from different parts of the world and from different schools and specialties to differ in their assessments of what women must do to create and maintain optimal health. I also expected them to be firmly attached to specific modalities and treatment pathways.

However, to my astonishment, when asked about the key pillars of health for women, *they all said essentially the same things.* And, when brought together in various conversations and health panels, they not only agreed, but fully supported and built on each other's recommendations.

Perhaps unsurprisingly, these recommendations have little to do with the latest diets, wellness crazes, or high-tech products; in fact, such solutions are recommended by our experts only in very certain cases for very specific health conditions, and only under the supervision of an experienced healthcare provider. Rather, the approach to optimal health supported most strongly by both the latest science and our experts' clinical experience is simple, timeless, and adaptable to exactly where you are in your life at this moment. Because, as with most things in life, the key to winning at health is doing small things consistently, on a daily basis.

The six pillars of optimal health for women are:

1. Enjoy good food that is good for you.

2. Incorporate daily movement.

3. Get adequate and restorative sleep.

4. Reframe and manage stress levels.

5. Tune in to your body's wisdom (and learn to sniff out the scams).

6. Find and work with high-integrity healthcare providers who will help you do all of the above.

As you can see, none of these pillars promise that you will "Drop the weight in ten days!" or "Eliminate your symptoms with one magic pill!" Nor will they "detox" your organs, or make anything "melt" or "dissolve." We all know that's just marketing talk. However, there are innumerable benefits to approaching optimal health according to these pillars—including their simplicity and accessibility, and fact that they work with your body and not against it.

By following these pillars, you can put in place a new approach to your health today. Everything about health in both the short and long term is linked to lifestyle.

In a world where we are saturated with miracle marketing and conditioned to seek immediate gratification, true pathways to health can feel decidedly unsexy and difficult to implement. And, as we've shown you in this book, the medical and wellness spaces are often influenced—and, dare I say, corrupted—by providers and companies who prioritize profit over people. Nevertheless, if we truly desire to create optimal healthcare opportunities for women around the globe (and we do), these pillars are the best place to start.

Each of these categories is adaptable to your current stage of life, health goals, geographical location, income level, mental health status, and any current health challenges you may be experiencing. Focusing on balancing and strengthening these pillars will inherently increase your health and vitality across all areas. Each pillar supports the others in both obvious and subtle ways.

In this chapter, we will break down each of the six pillars of optimal health and make some basic recommendations to get you started on your own journey. We have touched on much of the information in these pillars already in earlier chapters; this section is intended to bring it together into a cohesive picture for you, rather than review the details already covered. We will also provide you with tools to navigate the final two pillars—listening to your body and working with healthcare providers—so you will feel empowered to take meaningful steps in those areas. Of course, you will want (and need) to adapt each of these pillars to your unique health situation; this is where your provider partnerships can be highly useful. Therefore, the information we are providing below is in a summary format, rather than instructional or detailed.

While we can't (and won't) promise a health miracle when you prioritize these pillars of health and develop your personal "but can," we *can* promise that if you pull your attention away from the online fads and miracle marketing, stop the reductionist diets and extreme exercise routines that don't serve you, and put your energy into these six pillars instead, you will be well on your way to a better health reality.

Pillar #1: Enjoy good food that is good for you

The West has a two-dimensional understanding of nutrition. Nutritional "values" of foods are evaluated, and then recommendations are made according to those values. While it lacks nuance, this is actually a great start: if we, as women, only followed the most recent Western recommendations for diet and nutrition, we would reduce our chances of most chronic diseases by *up to 80 percent*. Yes, that means an 80 percent reduction in risk for Type 2 diabetes, heart disease, dementia, Alzheimer's, and more. Food is, indeed, the best medicine.

Eastern medical philosophies, including Traditional Chinese Medicine and Ayurveda, fully align to the Western idea of "nutritional value" but add many other aspects—like the benefits of combining (or not combining) certain foods, the effect that each food has on our bodies (cooling, warming, dry, oily, etc.) and the importance of food assimilation, to name a few. This view on nutrition adapts food recommendations to the individual's body type, sex, age, and health conditions, thereby bringing an aspect of precision to the food we eat. The goal is always to bring balance to the body and help it function at its best.

Here are some food guidelines that integrate both Western and Eastern wisdom.

Natural, whole foods are the best

According to the most up-to-date research about diet, inflammation, and longevity, vegetables, leafy greens, whole grains, berries, and legumes should form the bulk of your diet. Animal products like seafood, poultry, dairy, red meat, and eggs should take up less room on the plate. All sugars should be kept to a minimum.

Avoid trans fats and limit saturated fats, but get plenty of poly-unsaturated and monounsaturated fats (like high-quality olive oil, coconut oil, etc.), which can help reduce inflammation and support overall health.

Yes, good nutrition is really this simple.

Within these guidelines exist infinite food combinations, ingredients, and recipes. These parameters can be applied to any kind of cuisine—European, Chinese, American, Indian, Middle Eastern, African, etc.—without sacrificing health benefits. And while news headlines and influencer diets can make it seem as though scientific views on nutrition are always changing, they're only following fads; in fact, global consensus on an optimal diet for maintaining healthy weight and lowering disease risk has been growing thanks to a hard-earned body of evidence. In short, the experts agree that the simple guidelines above are, in almost every case, the best pathway to creating and maintaining your long-term health.

Diversity

Jenna Macciochi, immunologist and author of *Immunity: The Science of Staying Well*, shared the following with me when I consulted her about the food pillar:

> Dietary diversity is important for health because it provides a variety of nutrients and helps prevent nutritional deficiencies. When you consume a wide range of foods from different food groups, you are more likely to meet your nutritional needs for vitamins, minerals, and other essential nutrients.
>
> Eating a variety of foods can also help prevent

chronic diseases such as heart disease, diabetes, and cancer. For example, consuming a variety of colorful fruits and vegetables provides a range of antioxidants, which can protect against oxidative stress and inflammation, both of which are linked to the development of chronic diseases.

Dietary diversity can also promote gut health by increasing the diversity of gut microbiota. A diverse gut microbiota has been associated with a lower risk of chronic diseases and improved immune function.

Overall, eating a diverse diet is essential for maintaining good health, reducing inflammation, and supporting optimal immune function.

What it also important to understand when it comes to diversity is that too much of even the "best" foods or "superfoods" can be bad. For example, eating too much kale, broccoli, and other cruciferous vegetables can negatively affect your gut health, causing gastric issues like bloating and constipation. Cruciferous vegetables are also considered goitrogenic—meaning that too much over a long period of time may interfere with thyroid function.

Just as there is no miracle pill, there are no miracle foods. Each food has its place, and each has a job to do to contribute to your health.

Assimilation

Here is one piece of understanding that I've found to be lacking in Western dietary approaches, but which is deeply ingrained in the East: when it comes to food, it's not just about what you consume, but what you can *digest*. Many factors impact how your body assimilates food, including your age, life stage, immune system, lifestyle, and natural constitution. Learning to work with these factors will help you create a diet that is optimal for your body. However, these aren't the biggest obstacles to your body's ability to assimilate the food you eat. That honor, perhaps unsurprisingly, goes to stress.

Stress

Your body digests food most efficiently when your parasympathetic nervous system is dominant, sometimes referred to as "rest and digest" mode. If you are under stress (sympathetic nervous system dominant), even the "cleanest" and healthiest foods will not be properly digested.

Think of a time when you were preparing for a big presentation or had to have a hard conversation with someone. What happened? It's likely that your mouth went dry, your cheeks flushed, and your heart started beating faster. This is sympathetic nervous system dominance. Behind the scenes, your body also shut down digestion, shifting blood flow to your extremities in case you needed to run or fight.

Now, this response can be helpful in the moment, but over the long term it can wreak havoc on your ability to digest and assimilate food. When you live in constant worry and overwhelm, rushing from place to place, you will not be able to get the full value from the foods you are eating.

This is precisely why *enjoying* your food is such a big factor in health. Taking the time to eat, savoring each bite, is one of the best ways to ease your body into a parasympathetic state and allow your body to draw the full benefits from your food. Think of the pleasure of walking through an outdoor food market. You look at all the beautiful produce. You smell the earth, and the seasons. You come closer to the process through which we are fed and nourished by the earth. You feel hungry, and anticipate the satiation of a delicious meal. And then, you get to savor it all.

By focusing on only the medicinal or caloric aspects of food, or by following strict reductionist diets, we are depriving ourselves of one of the great pleasures of life: the joy of eating delicious, nutritious food with gusto. Eating is a beautiful thing—even a sacred thing. What changes when we lose sight of that?

In this way, mealtime is as vital to health as meditation, exercise, and good sleep. If you are following a diet that you hate in pursuit of health, you will actually have a harder time reaching this parasympathetic state and deriving the full benefits of your food. So, to counter the effects of stress on your digestion, eat a wide variety of nutritious foods that you love, and take the time to savor them all.

What can we digest best?

As humans, our teeth are smaller and our digestive tract shorter than many other animals, so it takes a lot of energy to digest and assimilate our food—anywhere from 10 to 30 percent of our daily energy, in fact!

This means that, contrary to popular belief, raw foods are often the hardest for our bodies to work with. Cooking and fermenting our food breaks down its components to states where we can more easily digest it.

When you are going through periods of high stress, life transitions, or times when your health is compromised (for example, postpartum, menopause, illness, or mental health challenges), it's best to provide your body the foods from which it can easily extract nutrition. Broths, soups, and other gently-cooked foods are essential during these times.

If you do not provide your body with foods it can easily assimilate, particularly during the life stages and events mentioned above, two things will happen. First, your body will not be able to extract the nutrients on which it relies; and second, you might develop digestive complications.

During times of stress, we may be tempted to turn to wellness products (like nutritional powders, protein drinks, and other supplements) to fill in the gaps in our nutrition. However, no matter how great the product, the nutrients in supplements will always fall short of real foods when it comes to bioavailability. If you aren't getting any green foods, a powder is better than nothing—but if you have the choice, always opt for whole foods prepared in a way that is gentle for your body. Whatever claims the supplement companies are making, their products will never fully replace or replicate the nutrients found in real foods, clean water, and sunlight.

Not everything is for everyone

Variety is key, but particularly when it comes to "medicinal" foods, not everything will be right for your body right now.

Here's a perfect example. Before moving to Asia, I had tried to integrate green tea into my daily routine, as I'd heard about its incredible health benefits. The thing was, I never felt good after drinking it. One cup would make my head feel heavy, and two or more would give me a headache and make me lightheaded. I thought maybe it was the quality or variety of the tea, so I bought the best organic, fair-trade, single-origin varieties I could find. It made no difference.

After moving to Hong Kong, I visited a tea shop and shared these observations with the tea master. He asked, "Do you tend to have lower blood pressure and low energy?"

"Yes," I responded.

"That's why. Green tea has the effect of lowering blood pressure, so it's great for those with normal-to-high blood pressure who already have lots of energy. For you, I recommend black tea—pu-erh, in particular. The fermentation process in black teas changes their effect on the body."

Studies confirm his assertion. A meta-analysis of thirteen trials found that drinking green tea caused a significant reduction in both systolic and diastolic blood pressure.[1] No wonder it didn't agree with me! I switched to black tea and have never looked back.

So it goes for all foods and ingredients. Foods can be beneficial or harmful depending on whether your body actually requires the effects—the "medicine"—they provide. Therefore, understanding how to adapt the foods you consume to your body type, stage of life, and even your hormone cycles can be extremely beneficial and help you get the most nutritional and medicinal value. This subject is so important to us that we've created many master-classes through OM to address it from multiple perspectives.

If you do nothing else, do this

What I've just shared may run counter to everything you've been told about nutrition and diet. You don't have to try to implement it all right now—and really, you couldn't, since it will take time for you to determine which foods actually work with your body and which don't support you. However, there are some changes you can make right now, today, that will create a tremendous improvement in your health.

Both Eastern and Western experts agree that, no matter what, you should avoid the following foods and ingredients:

- Refined sugars (meaning, sugar that doesn't occur naturally in the food itself. Fruits and sweet vegetables are great—so go ahead, eat that banana).

- Processed foods (meaning, anything prepared in a factory and designed for long-term storage).

- Artificial flavors, colors, and sweeteners.

- Highly processed or modified oils and fats, including trans fats like hydrogenated oils.

The above items, when consumed regularly, can be as dangerous to your health as smoking! If you simply stop eating these four things, and replace them with nutritious whole foods that you love to eat, you will make great strides toward health.

Pillar # 2: Incorporate daily movement

Movement is movement is movement. For optimal health, you should do some form of movement every day. However, what you may not know is that *it makes no difference what kind of movement you do,* as long as you do something each and every day.

For over twenty years, Professor Cassandra Szoeke of the

University of Melbourne has been working on and leading the longest-running study on women's healthy aging in Australia. The study has followed hundreds of women for more than three decades. Professor Szoeke told me in our conversation, "We assumed from the beginning that women who exercised the hardest and followed the strictest 'healthy' diets would be the healthiest in the long term, but that actually turned out not to be true, because ultra-hard workouts and diets are rarely sustainable. Instead, women who integrated movement into their daily routines are the ones who maintained their health. What found that just *fifteen minutes of movement per day* can add three years to your life—but you have to do it consistently. The same thing applies to healthy eating. Sporadic hard exercise, cleanses, and diets don't create the same benefits. When it comes to health, every day counts."

This appears to confirm and validate earlier findings by other researchers. For example, Dr. Chi-Pang Wen, lead author of a 2011 study entitled "Minimum Amount of Physical Activity for Reduced Mortality and Extended Life Expectancy," shared the following with ABC News. "The thirty-minute a day for five or more days a week has been the golden rule for the last fifteen years, but now we found even half that amount could be very beneficial. As we all feel, finding a slot of fifteen minutes is much easier than finding a thirty-minute slot in most days of the week."[2]

Amanda Thebe, author of the bestselling book *Menopocolypse: How I Learned to Thrive During Menopause and How You Can Too*, also recommends adapting daily exercise to meet your unique needs. Her suggestion is to commit to movement time every day, but choose the format based on how your body feels on that day. She calls this "structured flexibility." If you're exhausted, roll around on your yoga mat for a few minutes, and perhaps add some breathwork. Feeling like your energy is a ten out of ten? Head to that spinning class or do the HIIT circuit. Somewhere in the middle? A nice walk outside in nature will perk you up without exhausting you (even if, as we discussed in Chapter Five, you don't get in those arbitrary 10,000 steps). There is no right or wrong type of exercise, only what is right or wrong for your body, on this day, in this season of your life—and no app, program, or lifestyle guru can assess that for you.

So, unless you *really* love those hour-long weight training sessions, super-intense HIIT routines, or ten-mile runs, there's little health benefit to doing them. Training routines and fitness programs can be fantastic—but only if you feel good after doing them, can easily incorporate them as a regular part of your lifestyle, and most of all, enjoy them.

Pillar #3: Get adequate and restorative sleep

Some women are blessed with the ability to sleep anywhere, in any circumstance.

Then, of course, there's the rest of us.

Sleep can be elusive for women, particularly as we age. However, many of our most common complaints—like weight gain, hormone disruption, brain fog, and more—are directly connected to a lack of restorative sleep. If you can mitigate your sleep challenges, many of these issues will be dramatically lessened or even go away entirely.

In many ways, health and healing hinges on good sleep and adequate rest. Even the best food and exercise regimens won't support your health if you aren't sleeping well.

Let's recap some of the benefits of sleep.

- Sleep helps to improve brain performance and over-all mood. Put simply, your brain and body will feel better when you get good sleep.

- Sleep plays an important role in immune function and disease prevention. You actually make more white blood cells while you sleep, so poor quality sleep or not enough sleep can make it harder for your body to fight off infections. Also, good sleep reduces your risk of long-term health challenges like heart disease, diabetes, and stroke.

- Sleep is important for weight regulation, athletic performance, memory and cognitive performance, wound healing, and more. During sleep, the body undergoes a vast range of restorative processes that are essential for recovery and rebuilding. As you fall into deeper sleep, your muscles see an increase in blood flow, which supports the healing process. Also, the body produces proteins that facilitate new cell growth, muscle-building, and more.

How to improve your sleep

Sleep, like food, is a charged subject. It's common for women to feel frustrated around sleep—like they're failing in some way because they can't fall asleep, stay asleep, or sleep deeply. That's in part because women sleep differently than men. Women tend to have more sleep difficulties overall, take longer to fall asleep, and may have a higher risk for insomnia. It is recommended for most adults to get seven to nine hours of sleep per night, but more than 60 percent of women fall short of this recommendation.

Like the food pillar, sleep is a topic that could fill a book on its own—and, indeed, many experts have written extensively on the subject. Since we cannot cover the nuances of sleep and its integration with other aspects of health in detail here, we suggest that you speak to your healthcare provider(s) and/or a qualified sleep psychologist in detail about any sleep issues you might be having—particularly if basic lifestyle and routine changes like powering down devices early, reducing your alcohol intake, and creating a soothing bedtime routine don't help.

Pillar #4: Reframe and manage your stress levels

Stress has been proven to negatively impact every aspect of health.

The bad news is, you can't eliminate stress. It's a part of life, and it will never completely go away.

We keep hearing that stress has been proven to negatively impact every aspect of health—and while this is absolutely true, new studies show that stress is most harmful *when you believe that it is harmful.* A 2012 study titled, "Does the perception that stress affects health matter? The association with health and mortality," tracked 30,000 adults in the United States for eight years. Researchers found that people who had experienced significant stress in the previous year had a 43 percent greater chance of dying. However, that statistic only applied to the people who *believed* that stress was harmful for their health. People who were under a lot of stress but did not consider that stress harmful were no more likely to die than the control group.[3]

While changing your mind about stress can be a huge help, it's also great to have some stress management techniques in your daily toolbox. Many practices have the potential to reduce stress levels; breathwork in particular has been proven to instantly pull your body out of the negative physical stress spiral. For some people, intense exercise is as good as an antidepressant; for others, a calm walk in nature will be far more beneficial. In fact, a study conducted in twenty-four forests across Japan found that "forest bathing"—aka, walking slowly among trees without digital or conversational distraction—lowered blood pressure, cortisol levels, and pulse rates for participants.[3]

Meditation and yoga are also well-known and well-researched methods for stress reduction. However, there are as many approaches to these practices as there are people who practice them, so if you feel meditation or yoga might be helpful for you, take the time to try many iterations until you find one you can stick with. Take in-person or virtual classes, practice with free videos on YouTube, download a meditation or yoga app, or simply close your eyes and listen to your breath for a few moments while rolling around on your yoga mat. It all can work if done with intention.

Stress reduction can also be facilitated by more traditional "self-care" techniques like massage, energy work, a visit to the spa, or a long, hot bath at home. Remember, the mind and body are connected in every way, so when you care for one, you're also caring for the other.

Like food and exercise, stress reduction pathways work best when they are tailored to you—when they include things you enjoy, and are done regularly. So, feel free to try anything and everything that strikes your interest. Just don't allow yourself to fall for the miracle marketing pitches. No stress reduction technique will produce lasting results on the first try, and many—like meditation, yoga, or breathwork—may take weeks or months of regular practice before they reach their peak effectiveness.

Pillar #5: Tune in to your body's wisdom (and learn to sniff out the scams)

Our body is always giving us cues as to whether our approaches in the first four pillars of health are working for us. A huge part of health is understanding and honoring what our unique bodies need, and making changes when things are no longer working. However, many of us have been told for too long that we need to "push through" pain, exhaustion, or difficulties. We've been conditioned to second-guess our inner knowing and blame ourselves when the fads and miracle cures don't work.

In order to get the most out of the first four pillars of optimal health, we must deepen our relationship with our own bodies, and learn to discern what is truly right for us. Doing so requires us to do two things: listen to the cues our bodies are providing, and develop a nose for "miracle marketing" scams in all areas of the health marketplace.

Understand your body

Before looking at the "*what*"—meaning, the tools and pathways available to address your health concerns—it's vital to first explore the *why, where, when,* and *how* of your body, your stage of life, and your overall health goals. At OM, this is the basis of everything we do.

For example, in midlife (late thirties to early forties), your hormones begin to shift, including the hormones responsible for your hunger—notably, leptin and ghrelin.[4] When you understand the ways in which your body shifts during perimenopause, you will have a better idea of what to do next; in the case of midlife hunger shifts, one solution is to increase fiber and protein intake. What is *not* recommended is to go on a crash diet.

If you don't have context for or objective knowledge around the cues you are receiving from your body, it's tempting to reach for the "easy fixes" and fall for the miracle marketing. As you've seen throughout this book, that strategy often backfires. Therefore, it's worth your time and effort to learn as much as possible about what happens within your body at your stage of life, and with any health concerns you are experiencing. This will help you sort what is normal and expected (such as, to cite the example above, increased hunger in perimenopause) from what requires investigation or heightened concern. The more curious you become about what is happening within your body, the better able you will be to listen to your body's cues and put them into context.

Listen to your body

Throughout this book, we have touched on this pillar. Dr. McGregor has encouraged you to trust your knowledge of your own body when it comes to pharmaceuticals and medical treatments, and challenge your healthcare providers if you are not being heard. Tricia Yap shared in Chapter Five that diets that don't make you feel good are generally bad for you. And Amanda Thebe shared in Pillar 2 that exercise regimens should make you feel good and work with your life, rather than draining you or causing more stress.

Yet, you may still feel confused as to how to determine what truly works for your body and what doesn't. You're not alone.

Contrary to what we've been taught and the expectations that have been placed on us, it's *not* normal or optimal to experience fatigue, brain fog, inflammation, sleep challenges, digestive problems, or other issues on a daily basis. In fact, these are powerful cues that something in our body is out of balance.

Many women deal with these kinds of symptoms for months, even years, before seeking help. Instead of listening to our bodies and learning how to give them what they need, we soldier on, and accept that some level of discomfort or less-than-optimal function is "just how it is." As Dr. Jenkins explored in Chapter Eight, we start "forevering" our symptoms and learn to live with them instead of working with our body's innate intelligence to resolve them.

Learning to trust, listen to, and work with your body as a woman is a multi-layered and ongoing process. However, there are some simple ways to begin to engage with your body in a new way, and get curious rather than frustrated about the signals your body is sending you.

The best place to start? Your menstrual cycle—or your hormonal cues if your body doesn't menstruate.

Gigi Ngan recommends that women view their menstrual cycle as a "report card" on their overall health. Changes in flow, blood color, duration, and premenstrual symptoms can all indicate that something is amiss in the body, often before any other symptoms are present.

If your cycle is regular and established, you can use it as a barometer for anything new you add to your health regimen. For example, if you are working with a more aggressive exercise routine or a new diet, notice how it impacts your cycle. If it knocks your cycle out of balance (or makes it go away altogether, as happens for many women during intense training or keto dieting), chances are it's not the right solution for you.

If your cycle is irregular, painful, or sporadic, it's important to find a provider who can look at your body in a holistic way to figure out what is causing that imbalance. It could be related directly to your reproductive system—or it could be something else entirely! Once you correct whatever imbalance is occurring in your body, your cycle will also come back into balance.

Like your menstrual cycle, your digestion, sleep, energy levels, and elimination habits are also powerful clues about whether your current health choices are helping or hindering your health. Begin to pay attention to how you feel after eating certain foods (a food journal can be very helpful here), meditating, doing high-intensity exercise, taking prescriptions or supplements, or engaging in other health-related activities. If any of your daily functions are disrupted, chances are something you're doing isn't the best option for your body.

Above all, remember: it is not "normal" for the female body (or any body, for that matter) to experience pain. No one should shrug off period pain, menopause symptoms, body aches, digestive complaints, or any other complaint. When we do not accept pain as normal, we address it proactively and work to bring our bodies back into balance. More, we feel empowered to speak up to our providers and stop telling ourselves, "It's all in my head." It's not selfish to want to feel better. The quicker we address pain—any pain—the better we will be able to stop it from snowballing into long-term disease.

Sniff out the scams

The digitalization of health via the internet and social media is not bad, but it has made it more difficult to sort out the real science from the miracle marketing and predatory BS. Since there is so little regulatory guidance in this space, it's up to us to discern what might be beneficial to our health, what bears investigating, and when we just need to click "hide ad."

Intentionally or not, the global health market preys on women's pain. If you don't have a way to discern the hype from the true helpers, you will waste a lot of time, money, and effort on "cures" that don't work and may even harm you in the long run. Therefore, I suggest applying the following questions to each product, service, or treatment plan that comes across your path—including "cash for care" treatments through your medical providers.

- *Is this person an accredited expert in the field they are selling/speaking about?* If the person promoting the product or service is a celebrity, social media influencer, or even an expert speaking outside their field of specialization, look deeper and see what the real experts are saying before making a purchase.

- *Does this person have a vested interest in the product they're promoting?* This doesn't mean the product isn't viable. However, look for objective research and information before making a decision.

- *Is this person or company making big statements about "fixing" your health and/or suggesting that this product will "replace everything else you're doing"?* That's a red flag. No product, no matter how great, can do that.

- *Is this person or company pushing conspiracy theories or claiming that experts and science have failed you?* It's one thing to point out flaws in our healthcare systems, and quite another to sell a product by preying on people's fears.

- *Am I interested in this product/service/treatment because I'm looking for a miracle?* Understanding our own expectations can prevent overzealous marketers from taking advantage of us. Consider how each product/service/treatment can offer specific and targeted support in one of the key pillars of health. If that's not immediately clear to you, you probably don't need the product.

Pillar #6: Find and work with high-integrity healthcare providers who will help you do all of the above

As we've reiterated several times in this book, it's vital to find healthcare providers and professionals who listen to you, respect you, and are aware of the challenges women face in the global health marketplace. If your concerns are not being addressed with compassion, if you are not believed when you speak about your health, or if your lived health experience is being minimized in any way, that's a huge red flag that your provider is not the right person to partner with you in your health journey.

In Chapter Ten, Dr. Jenkins will elaborate further on the provider/patient dynamic and give you some highly actionable tools to assess your provider relationships, build on positive inter-actions, and seek out new providers if your current ones are not serving you in the ways you need and deserve. Dr. McGregor will also provide numerous tools in the upcoming Resources section to help you address and circumvent the shortcomings of the male-centric medical system and keep all of your providers on the same page when it comes to your prescriptions, supplements, wellness products, and health history.

As the African proverb says, "If you want to go fast, go alone. If you want to go far, go together." On your personal health jour-ney, you will absolutely go further when you have the support of aligned and knowledgeable providers. Your "healthcare team" can make the difference between a proactive, enjoyable health journey and one fraught with stress, hurdles, and suboptimal outcomes.

ABOVE ALL, BE YOUR OWN ADVOCATE

"A woman with a voice is, by
definition, a strong woman."

- MELINDA GATES

CHAPTER TEN

Finding Your Partners in Health

DR. MARJORIE JENKINS

Now that you know the six pillars of optimal health, your next step is to find aligned healthcare providers to support you in creating your best possible experience in each of those areas.

Working with providers can feel complex, especially for women. All of our conditioning gets in the way. For the reasons we've explored across this book—and many more that stem from our individual journeys—we hold back about sensitive issues when we could speak up, because we are embarrassed or don't want to be judged. We try to gloss over our symptoms because we don't want to be seen as weak, or because we're afraid we won't be believed. But these behaviors don't protect us; they harm us. Our silence and hesitation cost us our optimal health outcomes, again and again.

What I've learned over many years of working in both clinical and educational settings is that a solid patient/provider relationship produces the most positive outcomes. The groundwork for such a relationship is open, productive communication—and that channel goes both ways.

To help you understand the flow of an ideal patient/provider relationship, I've created this pyramid graphic. Building a great relationship from the ground up requires all of these elements to stack on top of one another—and, when they are achieved, positive results will ensue.

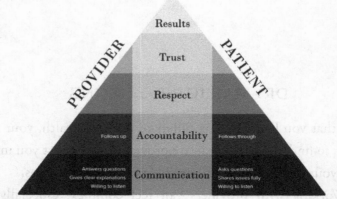

Results

Trust

Respect

PROVIDER

PATIENT

Follows up   Accountability   Follows through

Answers questions   Asks questions
Gives clear explanations   Communication   Shares issues fully
Willing to listen   Willing to listen

THE SUCCESSFUL HEALTH RELATIONSHIP

Note that both the provider and the patient have responsibilities in this model. If either of you cannot bring your piece to the table (for whatever reason), the relationship will be compromised and result in less than ideal outcomes.

Communication

As a woman, you have lived in your skin since before you left the womb. You know yourself better than anyone else. If you don't have a medical degree and can't use big, fancy medical terms, that doesn't mean you're wrong about what you sense in your body. It is your healthcare provider's responsibility to listen and learn from what you share about your symptoms, experiences, and health journey. However, it's your responsibility to find a provider capable of that kind of deep listening.

Then, it falls on both of you to communicate clearly and share complete information at all times. Although it may be challenging for you to discuss some issues or concerns with your provider, it is important to overcome your hesitation so that you can progress toward a clear diagnosis, improvements, and eventual results.

If you feel like your provider doesn't hear you, doesn't have strong listening skills or dismisses your concerns, the communication layer will be compromised. The same is true if you, as the patient, withhold information, minimize symptoms, or refrain from asking key questions. As vulnerable as it feels, the only way to test whether you will have good communication with your provider is to go all in and see how it unfolds. If, having done your part to lay the groundwork for good communication, you don't feel like your provider is a match, you should feel empowered to go elsewhere.

Accountability

Once you find a provider with whom you can communicate comfortably and effectively, you will move together through the territory of accountability. At every step, you and your provider should agree on mutual expectations.

Your provider should discuss your current diagnoses, their recommendations, and all next steps in your health journey. More, they should meet your agreed-upon timelines regarding research, testing, communication, and other explicitly stated expectations. In other words, if they say they are going to get you a referral to a specialist, order a set of bloodwork, or research an area where they need more knowledge to determine a diagnosis, that should happen in a reasonable time frame. You shouldn't need to spend lots of energy attempting to get information and feedback from your health provider, and it should not require multiple requests for them to produce information they have committed to providing.

On your side, accountability looks like following through—aka, doing what your provider has prescribed and recommended, and doing it consistently for a reasonable period of time. This means seeing the specialists (if recommended), getting the bloodwork done, taking your medications or supplements regularly and on time, and taking steps to change unhealthy habits that you and your provider have identified. Following through on these elements is part of your commitment to the relationship. The health pyramid is not one-directional. What this means is if you are unable or unwilling to do what's being asked, return to the Communication tier and have a clear conversation to agree on expectations.

If that doesn't happen, the relationship gets kicked back to the Communication tier, where you, the patient, can either begin again through clear communication or choose to exit the relationship altogether. Either way, you should feel empowered to take control of your journey to advance the progression of your health.

Developing empathy and building trust don't always happen simultaneously, although they are interconnected. Both take time.

Both are easily undermined. Both are the result of clear communication, compassionate boundaries, and informed consent. But while I consider it the professional duty of myself and other providers to bring an appropriate degree of empathy and trustworthiness to the table at all times, it's also our responsibility, yours and mine, as patients to reciprocate. If either we or our providers break trust or act without empathy, the foundation of the relationship will need to be rebuilt before those aspects are regained.

Respect

Like all else in the patient/provider relationship, respect goes both ways. Healthcare providers, by the nature of their expertise and role, are accorded a level of respect and—as we've explored elsewhere in this book—we have been subconsciously conditioned as patients to offer that respect freely. However, I have always sought to earn my patients' respect beyond my titles and credentials, and strongly believe that providers are partners in our patient's health journeys.

Respect is built through clear communication and accountability. By the time you get to this stage of the relationship, you should have established a rapport and demonstrated that both of you will follow through on your commitments. When this happens, respect is built naturally, and a feeling of partnership begins to emerge.

Trust

When trust is established, resistance melts. Each party becomes more willing to engage in creative thinking and revisit what isn't working. There is a perception that everyone is doing their utmost to create positive results.

Results

Health is about so much more than science.

As we've explored, the placebo effect has an immense impact on health outcomes. When women work with providers they respect and trust—and who respect and trust them—they are far more likely to experience positive results. When we feel that we are in good hands, we believe that we will get better, and that belief can influence our physiological responses to an astounding degree.

That said, trust and mutual caring should never outweigh tangible results.

Sometimes, women find healthcare providers they like and trust, but those providers are unable, for various reasons, to move the needle regarding their health. Some women stay with providers for years without seeing any sort of results, or even getting a diagnosis, simply because they have a long-standing relationship and trust them. In other instances, years of providers convincing women that their pain, fatigue, and other vague symptoms are not due to a "real" disease have conditioned women to accept what their provider says and not look for second (or third, or fourth) opinions. This is particularly common for women with conditions like fibromyalgia, chronic fatigue, endometriosis, and other health challenges which are not diagnosable by labs, x-rays, or other diagnostic testing. These types of health issues are often referred to as "invisible diseases"—and it's not surprising to me that women make up the majority of patients suffering from these conditions.

If you are working with a provider and do not see any improvement in your symptoms, it could be that you and your provider haven't moved through the stages from communication up to trust. (Note that seeing improvement doesn't necessarily require a diagnosis; for instance, the "invisible diseases" I mentioned above aren't thoroughly understood by science, and in such cases a diagnosis isn't necessarily a pathway to meaningful progress.) If your provider isn't helping you feel better, it doesn't mean they're not likable and trustworthy, or that they aren't great at what they do, only that they are not the best healthcare partner for you. Give yourself permission to find another provider.

The one exception to this may be your primary care provider (PCP). Primary care providers operate as a sort of "hub" within the medical world, and if they are unable to diagnose your health issue they will refer you to a specialist (or multiple specialists). In such a case, you may only see the specialist for a specific amount of time. Even if a diagnosis is made quickly by your PCP, you can consider trust to be the ultimate goal of the relationship. However, if you are being subjected to endless, inconclusive testing, if the referrals you are getting aren't working out, or if progress toward wellness isn't happening for any reason, it may be time to change primary care providers.

Above all, be your own best advocate

If you take only one thing away from this book, let it be this: change in the global healthcare marketplace starts with you.

Although it rarely feels that way to women on an individual level, the entire healthcare marketplace would crumble without our willing participation. When we choose providers and medical institutions we trust, who respect us, and who put people before profits; when we spend our hard-earned dollars on products that deliver more than "miracle marketing" promises; when we ask hard questions and demand better answers ... we are paving the way for change, not only for ourselves but for women everywhere.

If we want the best of anything in life, we must first refuse to settle for the inadequate, or even the merely serviceable. Seeking out the best that the healthcare and wellness spaces have to offer for your unique health journey across all pillars of health may require a bit more effort on your part, and may come with some short-term frustrations, but ultimately, the payoff will be well worth the time spent.

DR. ALYSON MCGREGOR

In the emergency department, one of the biggest challenges we face is getting a complete picture of our patients' medical profiles. Of course, modern digital medical records are helpful, and having information available at our fingertips has saved lives on more than one occasion. But, as you now know, conventional medical treatment is only a part of the picture of women's health.

Whether you're visiting an emergency department, your family physician, a specialist, a Traditional Chinese Medicine doctor, a nutritionist, or any other provider, you can markedly improve your quality of care by implementing the following three steps:

1. Educate yourself as to your health challenges, conditions, and history.
2. Ask powerful questions.
3. Provide a complete picture of your health information to *all* healthcare providers.

These factors will empower you to have productive, thoughtful, and meaningful conversations with your providers, and support you in building a foundation of trust and mutual respect with the right people.

I'll dive into these factors one by one.

Step #1: Educate yourself as to your health challenges, conditions, and history

Far too many women around the world take their diagnoses, symptoms, and treatment pathways at face value—meaning, they rely on what they hear from providers even when it doesn't make sense to them or doesn't feel true to their experience.

Even once you've connected with a trustworthy provider whom you believe supports your optimal health and will advocate for your best interests, it's vital to do your own research. Why? Because, in the end, it's *your* heath, and no one will be more invested in it than you. The more information you have, the more you can choose how to navigate your daily life to create optimal wellbeing, even if you're currently facing a health challenge.

Also, no matter how caring and thorough they are, your providers will likely not have the ability to give you a full, nuanced education about your conditions during your visits. Nor will they be able to provide (at least, not offhand) a comprehensive picture of all potential side effects or interactions from your treatments, particularly if such side effects are linked to uncommon or less-understood factors like genetic disorders, nutritional deficiencies, or hormonal profiles.

Popular information sites like WebMD, Healthline, and Drugs.com have solid information, but lack nuance, particularly around sex differences and women's unique disease pathways and health challenges. If you're looking to brush up on the basics about a particular condition or drug, these can be a good place to start; however, if you're looking for more specifics or a deeper understanding, I'd suggest going straight to the studies.

In the United States, access to the National Institutes of Health (NIH) National Library of Medicine—aka, PubMed, is free and open to all. Similar archives exist worldwide. In such collections, you can dive into medical studies published by journals and academic groups around the world. While some are complex and daunting to read (even for me, and I've published over eighty of them), the Abstract and Conclusion sections often provide key information that can help you ascertain whether the "meat" of the study will be relevant to you. When in doubt, bring the study to your provider and ask for clarification.

The FDA Drug Trial Snapshots database[1] is a fantastic source for information about pharmaceuticals. You can research information about who participated in clinical trials for each drug, learn about sex-specific and general side effects, and read the prescribing information.

You can also join online and in-person support groups for any particular conditions you are navigating. In such venues, people often share their health breakthroughs, what treatment plans (or combinations thereof) worked for them, and what they're discovering through their own research. The social dynamic of mutual support can also be hugely important for some women.

In short, the more information you gain about your own health—whether you are currently navigating health challenges or not—the more equipped you will be to approach Step 2: asking the right questions.

Step #2: Ask Powerful Questions

I love it when my patients in the emergency department ask me lots of questions.

In fact, I find that they are easier to work with, and often get better results, than patients who don't engage. Their questions show me that they are willing to have a conversation, learn more about what's going on with their health, and get curious about where their treatment could be improved. More, it shows me what they have, and have not, understood in our conversation thus far, and helps me fill in the gaps or rephrase my answers so that everyone feels clear at the end of the conversation.

I *especially* love it when they ask me questions to which I don't know the answers, or to which the answer doesn't exist! For example, I once had a patient say, "I know my stress test was normal, but you said it doesn't rule out other forms of heart disease like microvascular disease? How can I find out if I have that?" I then get to explain that we don't actually have tests to detect microvascular disease yet, and acknowledge that what they feel is real, even if it doesn't fit into our current diagnostic profiles.

The amount of information in medicine now is immense. That's one reason why we see so many narrow specializations, and why we are compiling databases of evidence that is searchable and edited by doctors. Up To Date, Epocrates, MDCalc, and other platforms can assist doctors like me in real time. If a patient asks me a question to which I don't have an answer offhand, I can easily search these databases to assimilate the information and modify my recommendations accordingly. Being curious is a *huge* part of my job.

Asking the right questions of your healthcare providers will open doors to productive conversations. It will also reveal areas where they have unexpected knowledge or interest, where they might have knowledge gaps, or—perhaps most importantly—where they might be incompatible with you personally.

As you begin to implement and explore the pillars of optimal health we identified in Chapter Nine, you will want to ask specific questions of your providers to initiate productive conversations around these pillars and find the best ways to support them in your life.

As women, there is another layer to our questions as well: a layer of self-advocacy. Since, as we explored in Chapter Two, much of our conventional medical system was not designed around women's bodies and needs, it is in our best interest individually and collectively to make sure that our providers are familiar with the challenges presented by male-centric medicine, and that they understand the unique demands of caring for, prescribing for, and proactively supporting the health of women.

If you are a woman of color, a gay or bisexual woman, a trans woman, or part of any other marginalized group, you might also choose to start asking questions of your providers around whether they are equipped to address your unique health concerns, if they have experience working with bodies and medical histories like yours, and if their knowledge base will support your unique health pathways. You deserve to work with providers who understand your unique challenges and will listen to your experiences.

In my first book, *Sex Matters*, I created a list of sample questions that women can ask their providers. (You can find an updated version of that list at www.Om-Experts.com/bookresources.)

Once you've started asking the right questions, you'll likely begin to get more satisfactory and actionable answers. The quality of those answers will also be enhanced if your providers have a complete and detailed picture of your health that includes all aspects of medical care, wellness products and practices, self-care, habits, etc.

Which brings us to ...

Step 3: Provide a complete picture of your health information to all healthcare providers

Many, if not most, women work with multiple healthcare providers in their lifetimes. Many see multiple providers simultaneously.

Digital medical records have made it easier for providers in the conventional medical space to access key information about treatments, surgeries, prescriptions, and lab tests, but this data collection space has not yet been expanded to provide a comprehensive picture of wellness, self-care, lifestyle, nutrition, sleep, or mental/emotional health for all patients. Sometimes, provider notes make it into the system as a result of conversations or diagnostic procedures, but more often than not, these areas show up as a blank.

Alternative medicine providers keep their own records—but these tend to be even less comprehensive or systemized, as such providers don't always have access to integrated healthcare or hospital networks. Rather, each provider has their own system by which they accumulate and reference patient information.

Fitness trainers, nutritionists, bodyworkers, and other service providers in the wellness space may have no records at all, or their records may be limited to what occurs within each session.

Expert providers in *all* of these spaces will be better equipped to serve you if they are working from a full and comprehensive set of data—about your health history, your ongoing symptomology, your daily routines and nutrition, the pharmaceuticals and supplements you're consuming, and your mental/emotional health. It's your responsibility as a patient to provide this information, and doing so in an organized manner will go a long way toward improving your quality of care on all fronts.

My suggestion is to create what I call a Personal Medical Reconciliation (Med Rec for short). This is a document which contains a complete and detailed list of all relevant information about your health and wellbeing. You can keep this document on your phone, on a cloud server, or even in your wallet. Share it with your partner, trusted family members, and anyone who has a medical Power of Attorney for you. Update it once or twice a year in general, as well as after each provider visit, and whenever you add a new treatment plan, prescription, supplement, wellness practice, or nutritional strategy.

To me, a comprehensive Personal Med Rec is one of the single best tools you can employ to foster cooperation and communication between your various providers.

Here are some basic information categories that should be addressed on a Personal Medical Reconciliation:

- Your basic identifying and health information:
    - Name, address, phone number, and date of birth.
    - Your sex at birth, current sex, and gender identity.
    - Your blood type.
    - The name and contact information of your current primary care physician.

- The names and contact details of all of your specialists, secondary providers, alternative health professionals, and wellness providers.
- The date of your last visits to each of your providers.

- Your female-specific health information:
  - If you menstruate, the date of your last period and your current contraception method(s).
  - Any recurring symptoms associated with your menstrual cycle.
  - Number of pregnancies, live births, and miscarriages.
  - Any complications with your pregnancies or pregnancy losses (ecclampsia, preeclampsia, cesarean sections, gestational diabetes, etc.).

- Current conditions and diagnoses
  - All current medical conditions and diagnoses (even if you're not actively treating them).
  - All current physical symptoms (even those not attached to a diagnosis).
  - All current mental health diagnoses, symptoms, and concerns.
  - Your surgical history.
  - Your recent tests and imaging, including providers.
  - Your current and past pharmaceuticals, including dosing and dose frequency.

- Your current and past wellness supplements, including brands, dosing, and frequency.
- Your current and past over-the-counter medications (like pain relievers, allergy medications, cold and flu medications, ear and eye drops, etc.).
- Any and all allergies (including to pharmaceuticals, over-the-counter meds, foods, colorants, and household chemicals), and your typical reactions to each allergen.

- Lifestyle and other information
  - Your current and historical alcohol and substance use, including natural substances and sacred plant medicines used in ceremony
  - Your (general) current and past exercise/daily movement habits.
  - Your (general) current and past eating habits, including any reductionist diets you've tried.
  - Your current and past experience in each of the key pillars of health (food/nutrition, exercise/movement, sleep, stress, listening to your body, relationships with providers), and which (if any) categories are presenting challenges for you.
  - Your religious beliefs (if they impact or influence your medical choices) and any specific personal requests you have for providers.
  - Your overall health goals and priorities.

I know this seems like a lot to put together, but once you've complied the information, it takes only moments to update it after each provider visit, screening, or change to your regimen. More, it will save you significant time when it comes to interfacing with your providers, now and in the future.

Here are some ways that having a Personal Medical Reconciliation form can support you in creating optimal health:

- When meeting a new healthcare provider, ask if you can share your Personal Med Rec in advance, so the provider can review it before your appointment and address your questions and concerns with greater specificity.

- Share your Personal Med Rec with your existing providers to make sure that their records are up to date—particularly concerning symptoms, prescriptions, supplements, and imaging.

- You can refer to your Personal Med Rec during appointments to reduce the chances that you will forget to share key pieces of information—especially if you are under stress.

- If you need to be taken to the emergency department, your Personal Med Rec can speak on your behalf, reducing the chance of errors or drug interactions during lifesaving treatments, and guiding providers toward the best follow-up care pathways.

As you can see, having all of your information in one place can support your health in all kinds of ways. To make this process easier for you, I've created a printable Personal Medical Reconciliation form with charts that you can download at www. Om-Experts.com/bookresources.

ANCA GRIFFITHS

Now that you understand more fully how to find, assess, and work with qualified and aligned healthcare providers, and create pathways to your personal "but can," I want to share more with you about the work we are doing at OM, and how what we are creating may serve your health journey in both the short and long term.

We—myself, Dr. Jenkins, and Dr. McGregor—created OM to be a precision health and health information platform. We built the company we, as experts in our unique disciplines, wanted to see and use.

The goal for OM is to empower women around the globe to understand how we work in all life stages and in all areas of health. Our focus is informed precision. We will never engage in fear-mongering or the polarization of health practices. Nor will we ever demonize any woman's health experience or treat any health subject as taboo. We don't sell products, supplements, or healthcare tools. We don't get paid based on how people take action on our information. Instead, we strive to provide the most current, unbiased, and scientifically-verified information and care pathways, and bring them to you through our global team of experts.

Our purpose, therefore, isn't to generalize your experience in order to sell products or services. Rather, our role is to cut through the predatory tactics and social media glitter to find the world's most credible experts in all fields of health and wellness. Their clinical experience and extensive education in their respective specialties means that you receive the best possible health information and advice.

None of our experts are mega-influencers. None rely on product sales or "cash for care" services. Never will this shift; just as we have done in this book, our only goal is to provide unbiased information so that women around the world can start—and keep—winning at health. What they do have is knowledge of cutting-edge information about health. And this matters when you consider that studies show that it takes seventeen years for new health breakthroughs to make it into routine clinical practices.

One of our key stances is that there is no type or genre of medicine that is inherently "wrong" or "bad." Western conventional medicine has a huge role to play in health, as do more holistic Eastern practices, "alternative" practices, and everything else in between. While every system has its flaws—many of which we've explored in this book—with the support of aligned and trustworthy providers, and the right balance of care, you can truly enjoy the best of all worlds and create a unique pathway toward your long-term, vibrant health.

ONLY ACTION
CAN PRECIPITATE
MEANINGFUL CHANGE

"Women are always at the
front of revolutions."
- **BUTHAYNA KAMEL**

ONLY ACTION
CAN PRECIPITATE
MEANINGFUL CHANGE

Afterword

ANCA GRIFFITHS, DR. ALYSON MCGREGOR & DR. MARJORIE JENKINS

Imagine a world where women's health is fully supported—from birth through the transition of death, and at every life stage in between.

A world where the global health market actually serves its consumers' best interests.

A world where women are seen, heard, and supported in every aspect of their health journey.

A world where miracle marketing and blanket "cash for care" are replaced by objective, relevant, and actionable information and precision medical support.

Together, that's what we are working toward at OM.

Now that you have seen the whole picture of the global women's health market, you will never *unsee* it. You now have helpful tools to research both traditional and complementary care pathways, vet "miracle marketing" claims, find aligned providers, focus on what really matters to your overall health, and advocate for your unique needs in clinical settings.

In other words, you are ready to start winning at health.

It is our hope that this book is the first step in a long and fruitful health journey for you.

Yours in health,
Anca, Alyson, and Marjorie

Endnotes

CHAPTER ONE

(1). Population Reference Bureau. "What Explains the Disparities Between Men's and Women's Health?" November 18, 2008. https://www.prb.org/resources/what-explains-the-disparities-between-mens-and-womens-health

(2). Westergaard, D.; Moseley, P.; Sorup, FKH; Baldi, P; Brunak, S. "Population-wide analysis of differences in disease progression patterns in men and women." *Nature Communications,* 2019; 10, 666

(3). Judith H. Lichtman, Erica C. Leifheit, Basmah Safdar, Haikun Bao, Harlan M. Krumholz, Nancy P. Lorenze, Mitra Daneshvar, John A. Spertus and Gail D'Onofrio. "Sex Differences in the Presentation and Perception of Symptoms Among Young Patients With Myocardial Infarction." *Circulation,* 2018;137:781–790. DOI: 10.1161/CIRCULATIONAHA.117.031650

CHAPTER TWO

(1). Livingston, Alex N, Mattingly, T Joseph II. "Drug and medical device product failures and the stability of the pharmaceutical supply chain." *Journal of the American Pharmaceutical Association*, January-February 2021; 61(1): e119–e122. DOI: 10.1016/j. japh.2020.07.005

(2). Lexchin, Joel. "How safe are new drugs? Market withdrawal of drugs approved in Canada between 1990 and 2009." *Open Med*, 2014; 8(1): e14–e19

(3). Bertoia, Monica L et al. "Risk factors for sudden cardiac death in post-menopausal women." *Journal of the American College of Cardiology*, December 2012; 60(25):2674-82. DOI: 10.1016/j. jacc.2012.09.031

(4). Garcia, Mariana; Mulvagh, Sharon L; Bairey Merz, C Noel; Buring, Julie E; Manson, JoAnn E. "Cardiovascular Disease in Women: Clinical Perspectives." *Circulation Research,* 2016; 118:1273–1293. DOI:10.1161/CIRCRESAHA.116.307547

(5). Brigham and Women's Hospital. "Heart Disease: 7 Differences Between Men and Women." https://give.brighamandwomens. org/7-differences-between-men-and-women

(6). McLean, Carmen P; Asnaani, Anu; Litz, Brett T; Hofmann, Stefan G. "Gender Differences in Anxiety Disorders: Prevalence, Course of Illness, Comorbidity and Burden of Illness." *Journal of Psychiatric Research*, August 2011; 45(8): 1027–1035. DOI: 10.1016/j.jpsychires.2011.03.006

(7). Zucker, Irving; Prendergast, Brian J. "Sex differences in pharmacokinetics predict adverse drug reactions in women." *Biological Sex Differences,* 2020; 11: 32. DOI: 10.1186/ s13293-020-00308-5

(8). Johnson, J A; Akers, W S; Herring, V L; Wolfe, M S; Sullivan, J M. "Gender differences in labetalol kinetics: importance of determining stereoisomer kinetics for racemic drugs." *Pharmacotherapy,* June 2000;20(6):622-8. DOI: 10.1592/phco.20.7.622.35180

(9). Butcher, B E; Carmody, J J. "Sex differences in analgesic response to ibuprofen are influenced by expectancy: a randomized, crossover, balanced placebo-designed study." *European Journal of Pain,* August 2012;16(7):1005-13. DOI: 10.1002/j.1532-2149.2011.00104.x

(10). Farkouh, André et al. "Sex-Related Differences in Drugs with Anti-Inflammatory Properties." *Journal of Clinical Medicine,* April 2021; 10(7): 1441. DOI: 10.3390/jcm10071441

(11). Greenspan, Joel D et al. "Studying sex and gender differences in pain and analgesia: a consensus report." *Pain,* November 2007;132 Suppl 1(Suppl 1):S26-S45. DOI: 10.1016/j.pain.2007.10.014

CHAPTER THREE

(1). Chinn, Juanita J et al. "Health Equity Among Black Women in the United States." *Journal of Womens Health* (Larchmt). February 2021; 30(2): 212–219. DOI: 10.1089/jwh.2020.8868

(2). Wu, Jennifer M et al. "Prevalence and Trends of Symptomatic Pelvic Floor Disorders in U.S. Women." *Obstetric Gynecology,* January 2014; 123(1): 141–148. DOI: 10.1097/AOG.0000000000000057

CHAPTER FOUR

(1). Sierminska, Eva. "Does it pay to be beautiful?" *IZA World of Labor*. https://wol.iza.org/articles/does-it-pay-to-be-beautiful

(2). Pollock, Samara BA et al. "The dark side of skin lightening: An international collaboration and review of a public health issue affecting dermatology." *International Journal of Women's Dermatology*, March 2021; 7(2):p 158-164. DOI: 10.1016/j.ijwd.2020.09.006

(3). Skalsky, Jarkander, M; Grindefjord, M; Carlstedt, K. "Dental erosion, prevalence and risk factors among a group of adolescents in Stockholm County." *European Archives of Paediatric Dentistry*, 2018. 19(1), 3–31. DOI: 10.1007/s40368-017-0317-5

(4). Mazure, Carolyn M, PhD; Schatenfeld, Nina PhD; "WHRY Offers Roadmap to Address Sex Differences in Opioid Epidemic." Yale School of Medicine, January 2021. https://medicine.yale.edu/news-article/whry-offers-roadmap-to-address-sex-differences-in-opioid-epidemic

(5). NSC Injury Facts. "Drug Overdoses." https://injuryfacts.nsc.org/home-and-community/safety-topics/drugoverdoses

(6). Howard, Barbara V et al. "Low-fat dietary pattern and weight change over 7 years: the Women's Health Initiative Dietary Modification Trial." *Journal of the American Medical Association*, 2006; 295(1):39-49. DOI: 10.1001/jama.295.1.39

(7). Park, Alice. "Weight Loss Supplements Don't Work for Most People, Study Finds." *Time*, December 2014. https://time.com/3648784/weight-loss-supplements

(8). Callaghan, Shaun; Lösch, Martin; Pione, Anna; Teichner, Warren. "Feeling good: The future of the $1.5 trillion wellness market." McKinsey & Company, April 2021. https://www.mckinsey.com/industries/consumer-packaged-goods/our-insights/feeling-good-the-future-of-the-1-5-trillion-wellness-market

(9). Freedman, Vicki A. PhD, MA; Wolf, Douglas A. PhD; Spillman, Brenda C. PhD. "Disability-Free Life Expectancy Over 30 Years: A Growing Female Disadvantage in the US Population." *American Journal of Public Health*, 2016. DOI: 10.2105/AJPH.2016.303089

(10). Schulz, R; Eden, J. "Older Adults Who Need Caregiving and the Family Caregivers Who Help Them." *National Academies Press* (US), 2016. https://www.ncbi.nlm.nih.gov/books/NBK396397

CHAPTER FIVE

(1). Hao, Da-cheng; Xiao, Pei-gen. "Pharmaceutical resource discovery from traditional medicinal plants: Pharmacophylogeny and pharmacophylogenomics." *Chinese Herbal Medicines,* 2020;12:2: 04-117. DOI:10.1016/j.chmed.2020.03.002

(2). Andrews, Karen W et al. "Analytical ingredient content and variability of adult multivitamin/mineral products: national estimates for the Dietary Supplement Ingredient Database." *American Journal of Clinical Nutrition*, February 2017; 105(2): 526–539. DOI: 10.3945/ajcn.116.134544

(3). NSF.org. "Supplement and Vitamin Certification." https://www.nsf.org/consumer-resources/articles/supplement-vitamin-certification

(4). Mohammed Basheeruddin Asdaq, Syed; Naseeruddin Inamdar, Mohammed. "Pharmacodynamic and Pharmacokinetic Interactions of Propranolol with Garlic (Allium sativum) in Rats." *Evidence Based Complementary and Alternative Medicine*, 2011; 824042. DOI: 10.1093/ecam/neq076

(5). Marzella Sulli, Maria, PharmD; Ezzo, Danielle C PharmD, BCPS. "Drug Interactions with Vitamins and Minerals." *US Pharmacist*, 2007; 1:42-55. https://www.uspharmacist.com/article/drug-interactions-with-vitamins-and-minerals

(6). Katz D L; Frates, E P; Bonnet, J P; Gupta, S K; Vartiainen, E; Carmona, R H. "Lifestyle as Medicine: The Case for a True Health Initiative." *American Journal of Health Promotion*, July 2018; 32(6):1452-1458. DOI: 10.1177/0890117117705949

(7). Lifestyle Medicine Education. https://lifestylemedicineeducation.org/

(8). Holtzman, Bryan; Ackerman, Kathryn E. "Recommendations and Nutritional Considerations for Female Athletes: Health and Performance." *Sports Medicine*, 2021; 51(Suppl 1), 43–57. DOI:10.1007/s40279-021-01508-8

(9). Calechman, Steve. "10,000 steps a day — or fewer?" Harvard Health Publishing, July 2019. https://www.health.harvard.edu/blog/10000-steps-a-day-or-fewer-2019071117305

(10). "Exercise: 15 minutes a day ups lifespan by 3 years. Exercise: a prescription for making your heart stronger." Harvard Health letter, December 2013; 24(4):4-5

CHAPTER SIX

(1). California Healthcare Foundation. "2022 Edition — Healthcare Costs 101." October, 2022. https://www.chcf.org/publication/2022-edition-health-care-costs-101/

(2). Vinogradova, Yana; Coupland, Carol; Hippisley-Cox, Julia. "Use of hormone replacement therapy and risk of breast cancer: nested case-control studies using the QResearch and CPRD databases." *BMJ*, 2020; 371. DOI: 10.1136/bmj.m3873

(3). Fresques, Hannah. "Doctors Prescribe More of a Drug If They Receive Money from a Pharma Company Tied to It." *ProPublica*, December 2019. https://www.propublica.org/article/doctors-prescribe-more-of-a-drug-if-they-receive-money-from-a-pharma-company-tied-to-it

CHAPTER SEVEN

(1). Mumcuoglu, Kosta Y. "Recommendations for the Use of Leeches in Reconstructive Plastic Surgery." *Evidence Based Complementary and Alternative Medicine*, 2014; 205929. DOI: 10.1155/2014/205929

(2). Jones, Brett D M, MD, MSc; Razza, Lais B, BSc; Weissman, Cory R. MD et al. "Magnitude of the Placebo Response Across Treatment Modalities Used for Treatment-Resistant Depression in Adults: A Systematic Review and Meta-analysis." *Journal of the American Medical Association Network Open*, 2021; 4(9):e2125531. DOI:10.1001/jamanetworkopen.2021.25531

(3). Wood, Frances A, et al. "N-of-1 Trial of a Statin, Placebo, or No Treatment to Assess Side Effects." *New England Journal of Medicine*, November 2020; 383(22):2182-2184. DOI: 10.1056/NEJMc2031173

(4). Meissner, Karin; Kohls, Niko; Colloca, Luana. "Introduction to placebo effects in medicine: mechanisms and clinical implications." *Philosophical Transactions of the Royal Society of London, B Biological Sciences,* June 2011; 366(1572): 1783–1789. DOI: 10.1098/rstb.2010.0414

(5). Fan, Xiaoqing; Meng, Fanli; Wang, Dahui; Guo, Qing; Ji, Zhuoyu; Yang, Lei; Ogihara, Atsushi. "Perceptions of Traditional Chinese Medicine for chronic disease care and prevention: a cross-sectional study of Chinese hospital-based healthcare professionals." *BMC Complementary and Alternative Medicine*, 2018; 18: 209. DOI: 10.1186/s12906-018-2273-y

CHAPTER NINE

(1). Onakpoya, I; Spencer, E; Henghan, C; Thompson, M. "The effect of green tea on blood pressure and lipid profile: A systematic review and meta-analysis of randomized clinical trials." *Nutrition, Metabolism, and Cardiovascular Diseases*, August 2014; 24:8; 823-836. DOI:10.1016/j.numecd.2014.01.016

(2). Wen. Chi Pang, et al. "Minimum Amount of Physical Activity for Reduced Mortality and Extended Life Expectancy: a Prospective Cohort Study." *The Lancet*, 378(9798):1244-53. DOI:10.1016/S0140-6736(11)60749-6

(3). Keller, Abiola, et al. "Does the perception that stress affects health matter? The association with health and mortality." *Health Psychology*, September 2012; 31(5):677-84. DOI: 10.1037/a0026743

(4). Robertson, Sally, B.Sc. "Doctors urged to prescribe woodland walks for mental health problems." *Medical Life Sciences News*, June 2019. https://www.news-medical.net/news/20190610/Doctors-urged-to-prescribe-woodland-walks-for-mental-health-problems.aspx

(5). Duval, Karine; Prud'homme, Denis; Rabasa-Lhoret, Rémi; Strychar, Irene; Brochu, Martin; Lavoie, Jean-Marc; Doucet, Éric. "Effects of the Menopausal Transition on Dietary Intake and Appetite. A MONET Group Study." *European Journal of Clinical Nutrition*, February 2014; 68(2): 271–276. DOI: 10.1038/ejcn.2013.171

CHAPTER TEN

(1). FDA Drug Trial Snapshots database. https://www.fda.gov/drugs/drug-approvals-and-databases/drug-trials-snapshots

Resources

Discover OM's expert masterclasses, corporate resources,
and more at www.OmHealthHub.com

Download all the resources mentioned in this book at
www.Om-Experts.com/bookresources

Acknowledgments

WE WOULD LIKE TO THANK all of the women with whom we have worked over the years. You have taught us so much about health—and, most importantly, why it matters.

Thank you as well to all the incredible health experts who are coming together to forge a new path for the health of all women, everywhere. We see you, we hear you, and we believe in you.

Our publisher Bryna Haynes deserves immense gratitude for her invaluable contributions to this book. She not only grasped the significance and purpose of this project, but also played a multifaceted role as our mentor, writer, editor, coach, and nurturer, ensuring that this book saw the light of day despite the obstacles we faced, including the pandemic, illnesses, and family emergencies. She welcomed us into her world, and her commitment to the project has been truly awe-inspiring. We are immensely fortunate to have worked with her, and her vision has elevated and expressed our message with the power of words.

ANCA GRIFFITHS

Someone once said, "Jump and the net will appear." I'm grateful to my coauthors and dear friends, Dr. Alyson McGregor and Dr. Marjorie Jenkins, who have been my "net" throughout the writing of this book and in our mission at OM. With their decades of experience and passion, they have tirelessly fought in the background to improve women's health, and for that, I and women everywhere are forever in their debt.

To my loving husband, Evan, and our two amazing children, Rupert and Emma: you are the center of my world and inspire me to be the best version of myself every day. Without your presence and support, none of this would have been possible. Thank you for being my rock and for being there for me every step of the way.

I was fortunate to be raised in a family where my father was always proud to be a "girl dad," and my mother instilled in me the importance of strength and bravery. Their love has lifted me up through every challenge and obstacle. I truly don't know where I would be without them.

I would also like to express my gratitude to Kristofer Richardson, whose talent, humor, and lightheartedness have injected life into all our work together. His experience of working with the top brands combined with his enthusiasm and support for our mission has been invaluable.

Virginia and Jeanette Sanchez have been an unwavering source of support that has enabled me to dedicate myself to this work day and night. Their care for our families has been exceptional and we deeply appreciate the strength and compassion they have brought into our lives.

DR. ALYSON MCGREGOR

To my loving and supportive husband, aka "logistics lead": you have helped me navigate my passion for women's health and uncharted career trajectory since we first met so long ago. Without you, there is no me.

To my loving and supportive family: I've said this before, and it's worth repeating. I won the lottery. I somehow secured the most supportive and loving family in the whole wide world (www). Without this foundation, I would not have the confidence to constantly move the needle further and longer on my road to career success.

To my Emergency Medicine community as a whole: the humbling clinical work we do during the best and worst of times, the grace with which we help each other evolve in our research endeavors, and the familial space we hold each other cannot be understated.

And, finally, to my co-authors: MJ, no other individual has influenced me more in my pursuit of a meaningful and fortunate career helping women. I am forever grateful for our friendship, collegiality, and shared passions. I constantly learn from you. Anca, thank you for providing a solution to fix our worldwide women's health problem! I feel our work will in fact be a critical piece of the complex puzzle, and one that can only grow.

DR. MARJORIE JENKINS

Thank you to my husband Steve and children Matthew, Katharine, and Rebecca, who have listened, conversed, and supported my passion for improving healthcare for all. My love for Steve and my three amazing children, and their love for me, are what sustained me during the most arduous times on my career journey.

I have a deep and abiding appreciation for all the national and international physicians, scientists, educators, advocates, and friends who make up my professional family. Marianne Legato, your pioneering work in leading the development of the textbook, *Gender-Specific Medicine,* and most recently in its fourth edition, was the first compilation of the science focusing on sex and gender in health. Reading the first edition in 2004, cover to cover, was a game-changer for me and would spark a lifelong commitment to providing personalized care for men and women through evidence-based medicine.

Former First Lady Laura Welch Bush, you gave me the most amazing gift. The builder of a research and educational institute under your name. The Laura W. Bush Institute at times felt like my fourth child, and I have always been in awe of your faith in me so early in my career. You also shared your wisdom along the way. When I came to you with the opportunity to join the US Food and Drug Administration, your words of support gave me the courage to go without the sadness that often comes with leaving something you love.

And finally, to my past and future patients: thank you for trusting and partnering with me on your health journey. I have and will continue to be infinitely blessed with the honor of caring for you.

About the Authors

ANCA GRIFFITHS

Anca Griffiths is the cofounder and CEO of OM, a precision medicine company where the best minds in healthcare come together to offer support and preventative therapeutic strategies to corporates and individuals.

An ex-luxury industry executive, OM was born out of Anca's own personal experiences after attempting to navigate the health market on three separate continents, which showed her the immense opportunity for credible and engaging precision medicine health support.

After working with the best and most brilliant minds in health from across the world, Anca was shocked to discover the extent to which women are the biggest victims in the current medical system. Working with thousands of women from across the world, Anca discovered firsthand the detrimental impact the rhetoric about the female bodies has had on our ability to meaningfully support our own health. She joined forces with Dr. Jenkins and Dr. McGregor, world-renowned sex and gender health experts who have dedicated their medical careers to championing women from inside the system. Together, they are working to ensure that women are empowered with the right information at every point of their health journey. Learn more at www.OmHealthHub.com.

DR. ALYSON MCGREGOR

Dr. Alyson J. McGregor is an is an internationally-recognized expert on sex and gender medicine and health disparities between men and women, and the author of the award-winning book, *Sex Matters: How Male-Centric Medicine Endangers Women's Health and What We Can Do About It*. Her Ted talk, "Why Medicine Often Has Dangerous Side Effects for Women" has over 1.8 million views.

Dr. McGregor has dedicated her life and career to changing the male-centric medical system from within to better study and support women's unique biology. However, educating medical professionals is only half the battle; the other half is educating the women whose lives are being impacted by that system. Learn more about Dr. McGregor at www.AlysonMcGregorMD.com.

DR. MARJORIE JENKINS

Dr. Marjorie "MJ" Jenkins is a well-known expert in women's health and sex and gender medicine. Dr. Jenkins has served in a variety of national roles such as Program Chair of the 2015 and 2018 National Sex and Gender Health Professional Education Summits and Co-chair of the Reproduction Work Group for NASA's Sex and Gender Decadal Review. She is a past member of the USMLE Women's Health National Board of Medical Examiners Writing Group and has served as an expert for HRSA and NIH. In 2007, she founded and served as executive director for the Texas Tech University Laura W. Bush Institute (LWBI), a research and education institute focusing on sex and gender women's health which now spans across six campuses. By invitation, Dr. Jenkins spent four years at the US Food and Drug Administration's Office of Women's Health as Director of Research and Scientific Programs. One could say Dr Jenkins "wrote the book" on sex and gender in medical care through her role as codeveloper and lead editor for the 2020 textbook, *How Sex and Gender Impact Clinical Practice.*

Throughout her career as a clinician, researcher, and educator, she has partnered with thousands of women to navigate their path to wellness. Dr. Jenkins has spoken for over 200 consumer and scientific audiences across the world. A top career and life goal has been to educate and empower health professionals and patients in refusing a "one size fits all" approach within the medical and wellness industries. Without access to captivating and accurate information, women can struggle to know who to trust with their health, and they suffer as a result. Dr. Jenkins believes it's time to change that.

About the Publisher

FOUNDED IN 2021 by Bryna Haynes, WorldChangers Media is a boutique publishing company focused on "Ideas for Impact." We know that great books change lives, topple outdated paradigms, and build movements. Our commitment is to deliver superior-quality transformational nonfiction by, and for, the next generation of thought leaders.

Ready to write and publish your thought leadership book with us? Learn more at www.WorldChangers.Media.

WORLDCHANGERS
M E D I A